MERRY CHRISTMAS and HAPPY NEW YEAR

Merry Christmas 1994

Amanda

Love, Jen

A JOYOUS CHRISTMAS

WITH BEST WISHES

A VICTORIAN CHRISTMAS

JOY TO THE WORLD

BY CYNTHIA HART AND JOHN GROSSMAN
TEXT BY PRISCILLA DUNHILL

WORKMAN PUBLISHING · NEW YORK

For our children, Thomas Ando-Hart; Jason Grossman, Roger and Christopher Bussell; Adam, Gita, Christman and Liza Dunhill; Emily and Joshua Tex.

And for our families and friends, who through the years have created our Christmas memories.

For their generous loans of Victorian buttons, jewelry, toys and other antique objects for our photographs, we thank Ilene Chazanof Decorative Arts (New York City), Nancy Marshall Antique Collection (New York City), Susan Hoy (Susan's Storeroom, San Anselmo, California), Karin Hassel (Fantine, Cornwall Bridge, Connecticut), Molly Blayney, Cyril Tunis and Starr Ockenga. For her thoughtful advice and considerable hard work, we thank Pat Upton. For his photography skills and consistently sunny disposition, we thank Steven Tex's mom and dad.

For the rich images and objects of our Victorian Christmas heritage, we thank the artists, craftsmen and printers who created them, the many anonymous families who cherished them generation to generation, and the antique paper ephemera and collectibles dealers who located, secured and offered them so they can now be enjoyed here.

For giving form and substance to the study of ephemera and its social importance, we thank the Ephemera Society of America (Schoharie, New York) and its president, William F. Mobley.

For their endurance and perseverance in transcribing the Notes on the Ephemera & Collectibles, we thank John's wife, Carolyn Grossman, and Irene McGill. For their gracious help and support, we thank Petra Koencke (Petra's Gallery of Flowers, Sausalito, California), Elisa Davidson, Harumi Ando, and everyone at Workman Publishing.

The photographic illustrations were created by Cynthia Hart and recorded on film by Steven Tex. All the paper ephemera c1820–1920 is from The John Grossman Collection of Antique Images.

Library of Congress Cataloging-in-Publication Data

Hart, Cynthia. Joy to the world : a Victorian Christmas / by Cynthia Hart, John Grossman, and Priscilla Dunhill.
p. cm. ISBN 0-89480-825-7
1. Christmas. I. Grossman, John.
II. Dunhill, Priscilla. III. Title.
GT4985.H312 1990 394.2'68282—dc20 90-50363 CIP

Workman Publishing Company, Inc.
708 Broadway
New York, New York 10003

Printed in Japan
First printing October 1990
10 9 8 7 6 5 4 3 2

CONTENTS

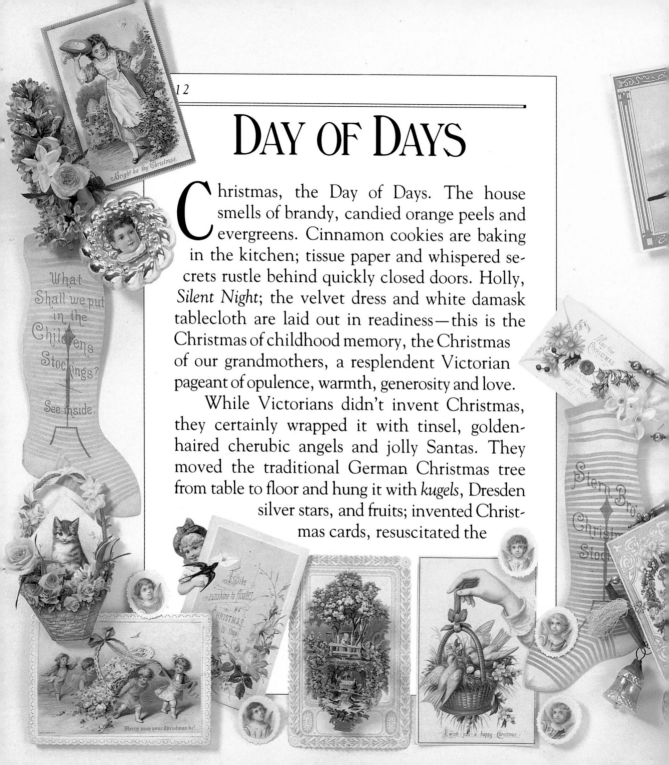

DAY OF DAYS

Christmas, the Day of Days. The house smells of brandy, candied orange peels and evergreens. Cinnamon cookies are baking in the kitchen; tissue paper and whispered secrets rustle behind quickly closed doors. Holly, *Silent Night*; the velvet dress and white damask tablecloth are laid out in readiness—this is the Christmas of childhood memory, the Christmas of our grandmothers, a resplendent Victorian pageant of opulence, warmth, generosity and love.

While Victorians didn't invent Christmas, they certainly wrapped it with tinsel, golden-haired cherubic angels and jolly Santas. They moved the traditional German Christmas tree from table to floor and hung it with *kugels*, Dresden silver stars, and fruits; invented Christmas cards, resuscitated the

Bright be thy Christmas.

What Shall we put in the Childrens Stockings?

See inside.

May the Christmas

Stern Bros Christmas Stoc

Like sunshine to flowers BE CHRISTMAS to thee!

Merry may your Christmas be!

I wish you a happy Christmas

medieval custom of Christmas carols, and ele-
vated gift-giving to a frenzied and delicate
social art.

But above all, the Victorian Christmas
was a family celebration. On this Day of
Days, children could be seen *and* heard. In the
1893 December issue of *Ladies' Home Journal*, in
a column entitled "The True Spirit of Christmas,"
the editors reminded readers: "Children are God's
own angels, sent by Him to brighten our world,
and what we do for these messengers from the
sky, especially at that time of the year which
belongs to them, will come back to us threefold,
like unto bread cast upon the waters." What
mother could resist that challenge?

So she joyously prepared feast and festivity,
decked the halls, and lit Advent candles to
symbolically welcome the Christ Child and
members of her own far-flung family.

*Like their prede-
cessors, valentines,
early Victorian
Christmas cards
incorporated
cherubs, love
messages, butter-
flies and flower-
spangled meadows
—all harbingers of
rebirth and the
new year.*

Stollwerck's
Princess
Chocolate

Stollwerck's
Princess
Chocolate

Stollwerck's
Princess
Chocolate

A Bright
and Happy
Christmas

Strangely enough, a bright and happy Christmas met stiff religious resistance in America. Although colonists had brought the Yule log and wassail bowl from England in the early 1600s, and the crèche and tree from Germany a century later, for 200 years a New England Puritan clergy had successfully maintained moral barricades against glittering Christmas festivities in the name of the Christ Child.

In his Christmas Day sermon in Boston in 1712, Cotton Mather had thundered: "Can you in your *Conscience* think that our *Holy Saviour* is honored by *Mirth*, by long *Eating*, by hard *Drinking*, by lewd *Gaming*, by rude *Revelling*, by a Mass fit for none but a *Bacchus* or *Saturn*? . . . . But shall it be said . . . that we take the Time to please the *Hellish legions* and to do Actions that have much more of *Hell than Heaven* in them?"

As late as 1846, in a pretty piece of sophistry, the Philadelphia Methodists advised parishioners to have a happy Christmas, "but not a merry foolish one devoted to mirth and trifling and mingled with sin."

Where, oh, where had Christmas got such a godless reputation? It all began with the midwinter pagan festivals of Norsemen and Celts; and with the Romans, who debauched during a midwinter feast called Saturnalia. For seven days, the Romans turned everything inside out and upside down. Masters served slaves; men dressed as women, and women as men. Courts were closed. No one could be convicted of a crime, and gambling was legal.

Saturnalia trudged into England on the backs of invading Roman soldiers, gradually metamorphosing into the bawdy and bloody medieval Feast of Fools. Reigned over by the Lord of Misrule, princes danced, drank, gambled and jousted—a celebration that much amused Henry

At right: an 1880s reproduction of the first Christmas card, designed in Britain in 1843 by J. C. Horsley for Henry Cole to send to his friends in London.

VIII and his daughter, Elizabeth, and just as much displeased English Puritans as frolics of the Devil.

The puritanical Roundheads, after beheading Charles I in 1642, banned Christmas for eight years in England; in America, some colonies followed suit, even outlawing the baking of mincemeat pies, a Christmas favorite.

In the nineteenth century, Christmas came tiptoeing into churches—through the back door, so to speak—when the American Sunday School Society began advocating Christmas programs for children. The Society assured a wavering clergy that a tree hung with a candy-filled cornucopia for each child of the congregation would attract 100 percent attendance, not

Hearty Greeting

A HAPPY CHRISTMAS TO YOU

MARCUS WARD'S

CHRISTMAS CA

ISVS CHRISTVS HODIE NATVS EST EX VIRGINE

WISHING YOU A MERRY CHRISTMAS

TO·THOSE·WE·LOVE·AND·EVERY·ABSENT·FRIEND·
ON·CHRISTMAS·DAY·KIND·SALUTATIONS·SEND

I sing a strain
With sweet refrain
A Merry Christmas
once again

May yours be a Joyful Christmas

The robin, a symbol of peace, was killed by
celebrants of the inside-out Feast of Fools.

the Devil. And what better teaching tool, to impress the story of the Nativity upon young minds, than a life-size crèche?

The crèche as a symbol of the Christ Child's birth derived from the fictitious but touching story of an adolescent Mary, great with child, and her gentle middle-aged husband Joseph. After a punishing ninety-mile journey through a barren, snow-drifted landscape, the couple arrived in Bethlehem from their hometown of Nazareth only to find that their sole refuge was a stable, offered by a beleaguered innkeeper whose hostelry was already overflowing. What is true is the stream of peasants, farmers and shepherds who journeyed each winter to pay their hated taxes to the Roman provincial governor in Bethlehem. The story of Mary and Joseph's tortured journey and humble lodgings was written a century after the historic birth with an eye to wooing lower-

> In the hidden nooks and hollows
> That the heart must seek for resting
> May the bird whose name is Peace
> Find a chosen place for nesting,
> Where its song shall never cease.
>
> —A poem about Robin Red-Breast by Helen Maud Whitman, from a card printed in Bavaria

Druids predicted the future from birdsong. Christians believed that the robin got his red breast by plucking the bloody thorns from Christ's crown on Calvary.

class Romans into the Christian fold, up to that time largely dominated by well-to-do intellectuals.

The crèche itself, like the Christmas tree in America, was of German extraction, come by way of Italy, where it had long been the focus of the Nativity. And no wonder! Imagine a small village in the Umbrian hills on Christmas Eve. The year is 1223, and St. Francis of Assisi is celebrating Mass in front of the open shed he has built and filled with life-size Nativity figures. Under a cobalt-blue sky bright with torchlight and joyful songs, the peasants, according to the writings of St. Bonaventure, fell prostrate with tears of wonderment before the first true crèche.

Immediately capturing the imagination of

Victorian Christmas cards often romanticized biblical figures. Here the Angel Gabriel, who brought the Virgin Mary news of her impending immaculate conception, drives a carriage of presents.

the illiterate peasantry, the custom spread throughout Italy. Even the simplest village possessed the raw materials to build a Nativity scene. By the 1700s, around Naples, the art of crèche-building had reached its golden age. Fancy ladies in their castles stitched tiny, intricate costumes, studding them with jewels, lace, and tooled leather. The costumes were fitted on terra-cotta figurines of shepherds, farmers, innkeepers, vintners, noblemen, the Magi, animals and birds, meticulously sculpted by the finest artists of the day.

The custom of crèches crossed the Alps to neighboring Bavaria and Austria, and thence to America with the Moravians, a German-born religious communal society. In Bethlehem and Lititz, Pennsylvania, these pietist religious pilgrims built such elaborate crèches—with waxen angels and life-size figures arranged in hillside settings—that farm families traveled miles from home just to see these outdoor works of art. Little by little, moving westward with German immigrants, the crèche crept into the heart of the American Christmas.

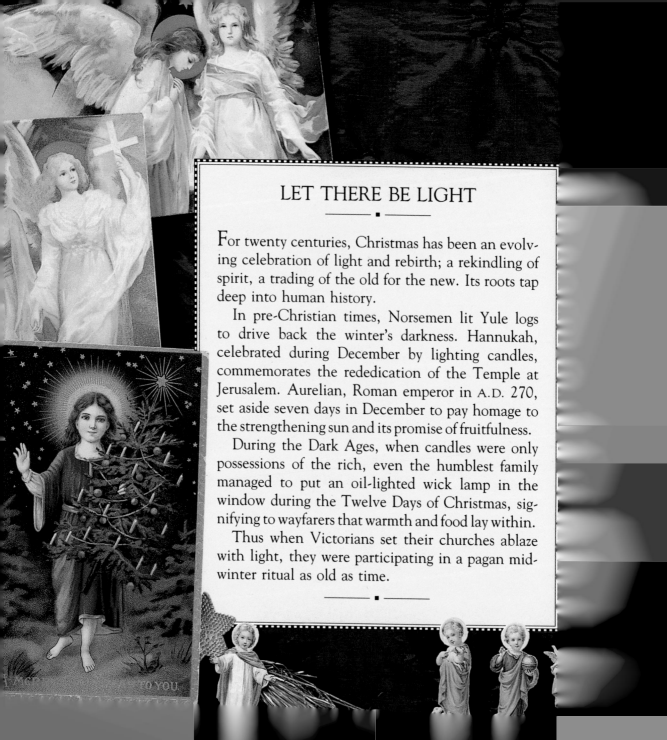

LET THERE BE LIGHT

———— • ————

For twenty centuries, Christmas has been an evolving celebration of light and rebirth; a rekindling of spirit, a trading of the old for the new. Its roots tap deep into human history.

In pre-Christian times, Norsemen lit Yule logs to drive back the winter's darkness. Hannukah, celebrated during December by lighting candles, commemorates the rededication of the Temple at Jerusalem. Aurelian, Roman emperor in A.D. 270, set aside seven days in December to pay homage to the strengthening sun and its promise of fruitfulness.

During the Dark Ages, when candles were only possessions of the rich, even the humblest family managed to put an oil-lighted wick lamp in the window during the Twelve Days of Christmas, signifying to wayfarers that warmth and food lay within.

Thus when Victorians set their churches ablaze with light, they were participating in a pagan midwinter ritual as old as time.

———— • ————

By the 1870s, most churches had become soaring caverns of light and music and greenery. Chancel, choir stalls, pews and narthex blazed with candles beginning on Advent Sunday. The great Gothic interiors resounded with the thundering *Messiah* chorus, "Unto us a son is given," and the sweet, pure strains of *O Holy Night*. Great music lovers, Victorians sang solos, duets and choruses in churches and upon any and all social occasions. It was inevitable that they would revive the jubilant medieval carols, which had spread across Europe from lonely keep to castle with traveling troubadours. The Victorian high tide of musical spirit culminated in 1871 with the publication of *Christmas Carols Old and New*. This compendium included the 400-year-old *First Noel*, sung in German, English

"**We** love all which tends to call man from the solitary and chilling pursuit of his own separate and selfish views, into the warmth of a common sympathy, and within the bands of a common brotherhood."
—*Thomas K. Hervey,*
The Book of Christmas

and French when the Victorians rediscovered it.

At about the same time, Christmas cards literally burst into bloom in England and America. As direct descendants of valentines, the first Christmas cards favored spring flowers and sentimental love messages — bouquets of pretty-pretty pansies, violets, forget-me-nots; sun-dappled summer scenes, butterflies, birds and animals. While valentines were sent primarily by young lovers, Christmas cards could be sent by everybody, as holiday wishes and a reminder that spring was not far distant.

In the mid-nineteenth century, Americans were ceaselessly on the move. Young people left the farms for cities, immigrants moved from east

Angels, according to St. Luke, in a burst of heavenly light, sang forth the joyous tidings: "And suddenly there was with the angel a multitude of the heavenly host praising God, and saying, Glory to God in the highest, and on earth peace, good will toward men."

to west, and everybody moved upward if they could. As the comforts of small-town intimacy lessened, sending cards was one way to fill the loneliness. Free city postal delivery, inaugurated in 1863, played a critical role, as did Louis Prang, German immigrant printer. Boundlessly confident in his new country, Prang devised a cheaper, less cumbersome system of printing color from zinc plates instead of the heavy lithographic

stones. His greeting cards became so popular in both America and England that the muckraking English press labeled them "a great social evil" for the burden they imposed on postmen.

Prang was relentless in the pursuit of quality, sponsoring art and poetry competitions with $1,000 and $2,000 prizes, and by 1881 five million of his cards were sold each year. As Victorianism moved into the Gilded Age, cards became more and more elaborate, with silk fringe, lace, satin centers perfumed with sachet, tinsel, feathers, foldouts and pop-ups. Animated cards came into vogue — one pull of a tab set three groups of figures moving against a backdrop of gilt and lace. But always, no matter how lavish the presentation, the holiday sentiment was paramount.

DECK THE HALLS

In the dim glow of a too-early Christmas morning, wriggling children dance attendance as Pa in his slippers and Ma in her cap roll back the big, polished double mahogany parlor doors. *Magnificat! Gloria in Excelsis Deo! Celestial!* The Victorian Christmas tree is as close to heaven as one can get on earth!

It stands on the floor, a regal, gift-laden glory, twinkling with candles, lacquered Santas, spun-glass fairy angels, chocolate wreaths, gilded apples, silver cornucopias dripping with silken tassels, glazed cherries and sugarplums. Every branch is adorned with memories and love: gingerbread men, wind-up trinkets, tin soldiers, whistles, homemade gifts and homemade ornaments treasured over the years.

The Christmas tree arrived in England with King George I, whose native Germany originated the custom. At age thirteen his great-great-granddaughter, Victoria, dutifully recorded in her diary — as she did everything — that she had seen two tabletop Christmas trees in her uncle's royal drawing room. But it was the famous etching of the Royal Family in the *Illustrated News*, showing Victoria the Queen, her German-born consort, Prince Albert, and their children gathered around their Christmas tree in Windsor Castle, that catapulted the tree into Victorian fashionability. Soon the *au courant* of London, always quick to emulate the trend-setting Queen, were buying "Royal" Christmas trees in the Covent Garden markets. The etching, originally printed in 1848, was reproduced two years later in the influential *Godey's Lady's Book*, published in Philadelphia. Editor Sarah Hale democratized the etching, removing Victoria's crown and Albert's chest-ribbon full of medals.

CHRISTMAS COTTON

The first cotton-batting Santas and angels were made at home, where every housewife worth her salt kept a goodly supply of batting for stuffing quilts. On November evenings, mothers cut the stiff cardboard backing for the children, who decorated the batting with shiny "scrap" faces, golden angel's wings, cloves for Santa's buttons and red velvet with rabbit fur for his cape.

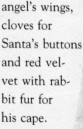

Tree decorations were homespun and homemade. Sugarplums, gingerbread Santas, or strings of dried apple slices called "schnitz" were tied to the tree.

The Christmas tree arrived in America in the nineteenth century. That story begins in the 1300s, in northern Europe, when performers strolled the streets bearing huge pine boughs laden with apples. As walking advertisements for the miracle plays they staged on the church steps, the boughs represented the Garden of Eden in the play of Adam and Eve, traditionally performed on December 24. Gradually this "paradise" tree, as it was called, transmuted into a tree of life—the Christ Child's tree.

One of the first written references to a Christmas tree was in 1605 in Strasbourg, where a visitor reported seeing a tree decorated with apples, gilded candies, paper roses and thin wafers. The rose was the symbol of the Virgin Mary; the wafers represented the host of Holy Communion, and the gilded candies were for children. The writer called the tree *Christbaum*.

Two hundred years later, such a tree was

In 1810, artist John Lewis Kimmell of Philadelphia sketched his family around a German tabletop tree. The tannenbaum took instant hold of the hearts of Victorians. By 1900, the U.S. Forest Service estimated that one family in five had a Christmas tree.

By 1890 the thin-walled, mold-blown figural ornaments were so popular that the glassblowers of Lauscha, Germany, could not fill the demand. That year F. W. Woolworth cornered the market, ordering 200,000 ornaments for his 13 stores.

With Christmas Compliments FROM THE Woolson Spice Co.

A MERRY CHRISTMAS & A HAPPY NEW YEAR

A HAPPY NEW YEAR

Unter dem Weihnachtsbaum.

A MERRY CHRISTMAS

Christmas-day with mirth and pleasure
Comes again with wonted treasure,
Filling each heart with delight.
Decking all the Earth in white.
Every kind of joyous play
Glads our hearts on Christmas-day.
That it may be yet more pleasant
Please accept this little present.

brought to America by Germans settling in Pennsylvania. By 1848, the beloved little firs were selling in Philadelphia markets.

While the idea of the Christmas tree originated in Germany, it was mercantile New York City that promoted it. In 1851, a Catskills woodsman, Mark Carr, loaded pine trees on a Hudson River steamer to sell them from New York City docks. His wife thought the venture a risky business. Two days later he came home with his pockets full of money—as did he and his sons for the next thirty years. By 1880 there were 400 tree merchants in New York City, selling about 40 miles of evergreen rope and 200,000 trees annually.

The problem was rapidly becoming one of supply, not demand. As the Catskills region was denuded of evergreens, imports from Connecticut, Massachusetts and Maine allowed the Victorians to indulge their madness for Christmas trees. In 1901, the year conservationist Teddy Roosevelt refused to have a Christmas tree in the White House, the first Christmas tree farm was planted near Trenton, New Jersey.

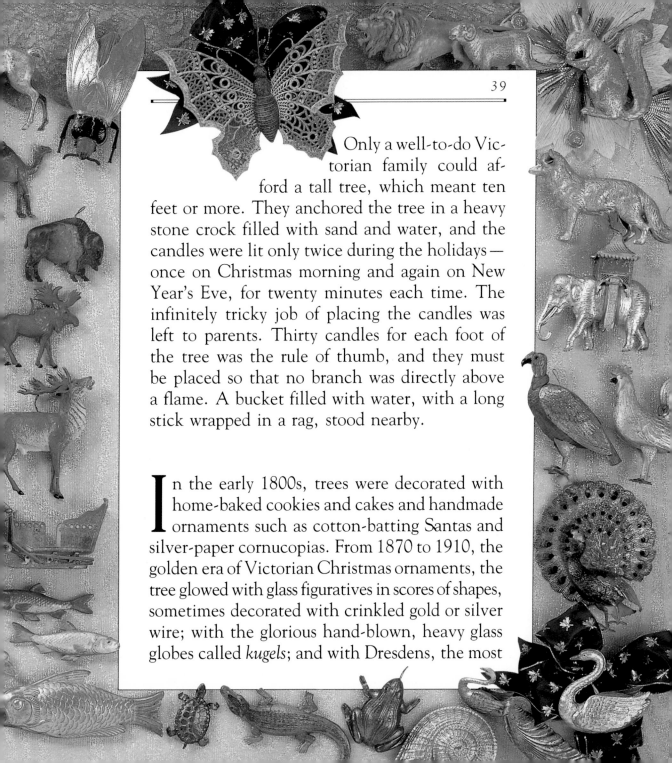

Only a well-to-do Victorian family could afford a tall tree, which meant ten feet or more. They anchored the tree in a heavy stone crock filled with sand and water, and the candles were lit only twice during the holidays — once on Christmas morning and again on New Year's Eve, for twenty minutes each time. The infinitely tricky job of placing the candles was left to parents. Thirty candles for each foot of the tree was the rule of thumb, and they must be placed so that no branch was directly above a flame. A bucket filled with water, with a long stick wrapped in a rag, stood nearby.

In the early 1800s, trees were decorated with home-baked cookies and cakes and handmade ornaments such as cotton-batting Santas and silver-paper cornucopias. From 1870 to 1910, the golden era of Victorian Christmas ornaments, the tree glowed with glass figuratives in scores of shapes, sometimes decorated with crinkled gold or silver wire; with the glorious hand-blown, heavy glass globes called *kugels*; and with Dresdens, the most

A merry Christmas.

Come under the mistletoe.

A happy Christmas.

exquisite paper ornaments ever created. Produced in delicate detail, the Dresdens appeared to be etched silver and gold in the glint of candlelight. German artisans handcrafted these elegant three-dimensional animals, moons, beetles, butterflies, turtles and fish. (Carp was a German Christmas delicacy.) Keeping up with the times, by the turn of the century these paper magicians were turning out steamships, autos and airships. In a simple but labor-intensive process, embossed cardboard, gold and silver foil, paper and glue were steam-pressed between negative and positive molds; when the two halves had dried, they were decorated, then painstakingly assembled by hand.

In addition to the Dresdens, Nuremberg angels were prized tree ornaments. Named after her place of

TREE SWEETS

The German Christmas tree dainty called marzipan was shaped into animals, Santas, angels and even musical instruments. The possibilities were endless, since the dough—sugar, egg whites and almond paste—could be so easily molded. If the marzipan was not to be eaten, frugal German *hausfrauen* substituted wheat flour and glue for the costly almond paste.

origin, a Nuremberg angel wore a crinkled gold skirt, spun-glass wings, and a sweet innocent face made of wax or clay bisque. Sometimes she carried a silver-lettered scroll that read "Peace on Earth" as she spun round and round, suspended over the tree.

Her place of honor atop the tree reflected an evolution of some 3,000 years. In paintings and manuscripts, angels bathed in heavenly light had long been message bearers of the gods. Greeks and Romans gave them wings. Hebrews in the Old Testament ranked them in a descending hierarchy, according to their closeness to God: seraphim and cherubim, then archangels, and finally the lowest order, angels who appeared only to man. According to the Gospel of St. Luke, written about A.D. 80, the Angel Gabriel appeared to Mary to announce that she would bear the Christ Child. By the fourth century, angels were an accepted part of Christian convention.

The crossover of the angel of biblical antiquity into the dazzling Victorian panoply of Christmas was natural. With golden ringlets and rosy-cheeked innocence, children were beloved

Poinsettias, poetically called "flame flowers of the Holy Night" in their native Mexico, became the nation's Christmas flower in the 1920s when the Ecke family of southern California developed a potted hybrid.

Sing to the
the Christmas Holly,
Holly.
That hangs over peasant
and king;
While we laugh and carouse
'neath its glittering boughs,
To the Christmas
Holly
we'll sing.
Eliza Cook.

MAY.   JUNE.
S. 1 8 15 22 29   S. 5 12 19 26
M. 2 9 16 23 30   M. 6 13 20 27
T. 3 10 17 24 31   T. 7 14 21 28
W. 4 11 18 25   W. 1 8 15
T. 5 12 19 26   T. 2 9 16
F. 6 13 20 27   F. 3 10 17
S. 7 14 21 28   S. 4 11

MARCH.   APRIL.
S. 6 13 20 27   S. 3 10 17 24
M. 7 14 21 28   M. 4 11 18 25
T. 1 8 15 22 29 T. 5 12 19 26
W. 2 9 16 23 30 W. 6 13 20 27
T. 3 10 17 24 31 T. 7 14 21 28
F. 4 11 18 25   F. 1 8 15 22 29
S. 5 12 19 26   S. 2 9 16 23 30

1899

JANUARY.   FEBRUARY.
S. 1 8 15 22 29   S. 5 12 19 26
M. 2 9 16 23 30   M. 6 13 20 27
T. 3 10 17 24 31   T. 7 14 21 28
W. 4 11 18 25   W. 1 8 15 22
T. 5 12 19 26   T. 2 9 16 23
F. 6 13 20 27   F. 3 10 17 24
S. 7 14 21 28   S. 4 11 18 25

But give me holly,
Bold and jolly,
Honest, prickly,
Shining holly.
Pluck me holly
Leaf and berry
For the day when
I make merry.

—Christina Rossetti

by Victorians. As delicate, ethereal creatures of purity and grace, angels personified the Victorian vision of the Ideal Woman.

While the tree was usually installed the night before Christmas, decorating the house began mid-December with the family trip to market to buy armloads of greens from street pushcarts— spruce, balsam, laurel, cedar, ivy, mistletoe, holly, and yards and yards of evergreen rope if you were rich. If not, you made your own at home, twisting the boughs around picture frames, over the oak sideboard where the best family china was kept, up and down banisters, or shaping a Gothic arch between the parlors.

After every square inch of wooden surface had been garlanded and wreathed, the mistress of the house went off to decorate the church. As a

STOCKING SURPRISES

The origin of hanging Christmas stockings is obscure, but prevailing legend attributes the custom to St. Nicholas, patron saint of children and maidens. St. Nick, so the story goes, tossed gold coins down the chimney of three sisters, doomed to spinsterhood for want of a dowery. The coins, fortuitously, were netted by the maidens' stockings hung to dry by the fire.

In Europe, St. Nicholas filled children's shoes (not stockings) with switches or candies, punishing the bad and rewarding the good.

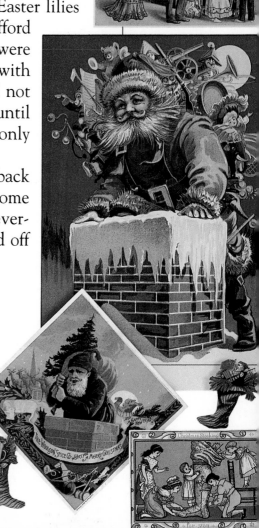

member of the church beautification commit-tee, she hung swags of green along the altar rail, made a boxwood cross or a star of laurel leaves for the pulpit. The chancel was banked with white lilies, the kind we call Easter lilies today. If the congregation could afford them, red roses or red carnations were added. The poinsettia of Mexico, with its rosettes of bright-red bracts, did not appear on the American market until the turn of the century, and then only as a cut-flower novelty.

The hanging of greens stretches back before written history. Folktales come down to us of Norsemen pinning ever-green boughs over doorways to ward off

CHRISTMAS EVE—HANGING UP THE STOCKINGS.

evil. The greens were also taken indoors to freshen stale air and to freshen spirits during the long, drear winter. And early in the seventh century, facing stiff competition from the long-established Anglo-Saxon religious cults in England, Pope Gregory I instructed Augustine of Canterbury to incorporate any and all pagan customs into the Church—including the hanging of greens as long as it brought in converts.

Seldom did Victorians realize, as they decked their halls, that they participated in the ritual of hope and renewal as surely as their forefathers had done down the long corridor of human history.

Fulfilling "visions of sugarplums" was the cheery province of mothers, cooed the editor of "The Mother's Corner" in November 1890.

A CHRISTMAS DREAM.

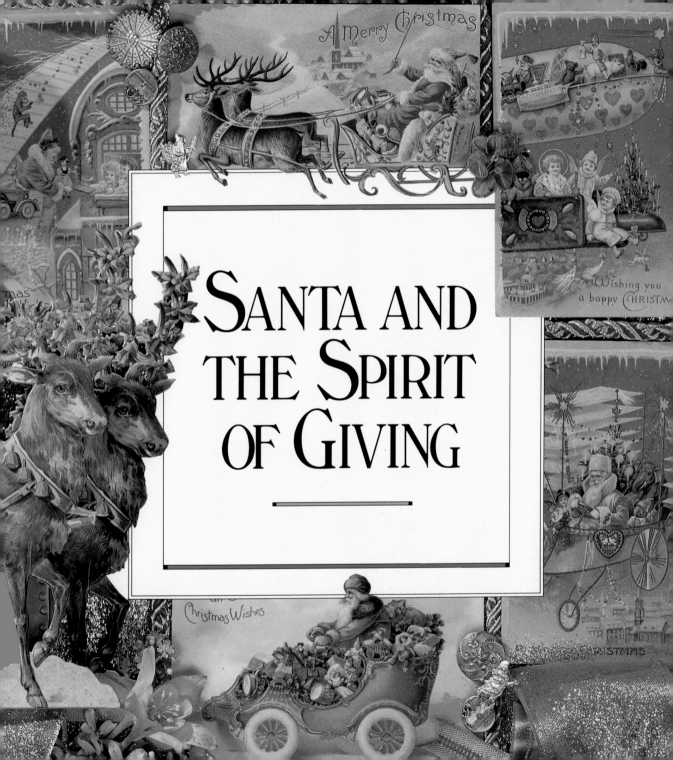

SANTA AND THE SPIRIT OF GIVING

The English gave us wassail and holly and Father Christmas; the Germans, *kugels* and Christmas trees; the Norsemen, mistletoe and the Yule log. But American Victorians gave us Santa Claus, chubby-cheeked, jolly and red-suited, a uniquely American folk creature of goodwill and prosperity.

While Santas in the guise of Father Christmas, Père Noël, Kriss Kringle and St. Nicholas have been trudging over the globe for many centuries, there is not a scrap of historical evidence that any of them ever really existed. These mythical Santas have survived because theirs is a legend so magical, and so bewitching, that time has given them the power of truth.

Our Santa's legendary antecedent came from the frozen wastelands of the Vikings and Visigoths, where he took the form of the Norse god Odin, a tall, truculent-looking fellow with a long, flowing beard. His elfin helpers were clad in tattered browns and greens—a perfect camouflage in the impenetrable Nordic forests, thick with trees and evil spirits. Odin's direct descendant was the English Father Christmas, gaunt, wearing a brown hooded cape, which in

later years was colored green or black or blue. Crowned with sprigs of holly, Father Christmas upon occasion got roaring drunk as he traveled about the countryside on foot or astride a white goat, stopping off at lodges and cottages to deliver gifts or share his wassail bowl filled with Christmas spirits.

In Germany the hooded cape of Father Christmas turned into a necessity for Pelz Nichol (which, in German, literally means "Santa in Fur") on his rounds in the harsher winters of northern Europe. (*Kriss Kringle*, the German name for Santa, is an eighteenth-century Americanization of *Christkindl*, or Christ Child.)

In the Lowlands, that seabound part of Europe which is now the Netherlands and Belgium, St. Nicholas, as patron saint of seafarers, was garbed in the sumptuous bishop's robes of his

SEASON'S GREETINGS

Queen Victoria's Christmas card for 1893, reported *Home Chat*, was "not only procured at great expense for all her royal relatives . . . but she buys not less than thousands to send to her neighbours at Windsor and Osborne, plus 100 standing cards, 12 inches high, with Wise Men offering gifts to the infant saviour."

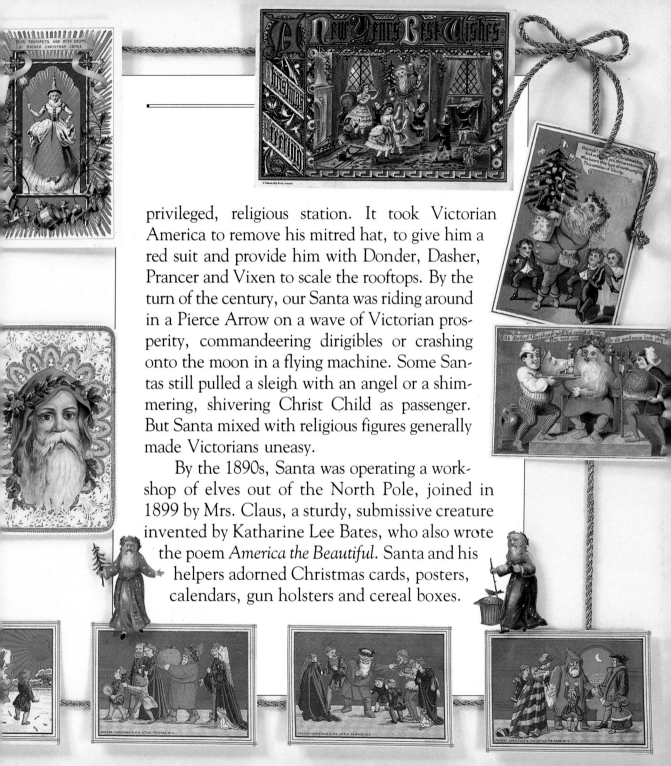

privileged, religious station. It took Victorian America to remove his mitred hat, to give him a red suit and provide him with Donder, Dasher, Prancer and Vixen to scale the rooftops. By the turn of the century, our Santa was riding around in a Pierce Arrow on a wave of Victorian prosperity, commandeering dirigibles or crashing onto the moon in a flying machine. Some Santas still pulled a sleigh with an angel or a shimmering, shivering Christ Child as passenger. But Santa mixed with religious figures generally made Victorians uneasy.

By the 1890s, Santa was operating a workshop of elves out of the North Pole, joined in 1899 by Mrs. Claus, a sturdy, submissive creature invented by Katharine Lee Bates, who also wrote the poem *America the Beautiful*. Santa and his helpers adorned Christmas cards, posters, calendars, gun holsters and cereal boxes.

They befriended the downtrodden and poor in spirit and were hung in joyous effigy from doorjambs, chandeliers and tree branches. Sometimes Santa curled up with a snifter of brandy, sometimes with kittens, sometimes with cherubic children or Mother Goose characters.

Three Victorians molded Santa into his present image of jolly gift-giver. Washington Irving, in his *History of New York*, described a jovial St. Nicholas who was carved into the prow of a boat coming to the New World. In Nieuw Amsterdam, the good St. Nick commandeers a wagon and flies over the snowy Hudson Valley on St. Nicholas Day, dropping gifts down chimneys to his favorites. (St. Nicholas did indeed arrive in the New World in the 1620s, but after 1700 no mention is made of him in New Amsterdam, now New York. Like Rip Van Winkle,

take these Xmas cards.

THE ORIGINAL ST. NICK

The granddaddy of all Santas was the young bishop Nicholas, who lived in the seaport of Myra in present-day Turkey. He delivered alms to the poor and small gifts to the children, defending Christianity when it cost one's life to do so. In twelfth-century France on St. Nicholas Day, when nuns resurrected the custom of gifts for children, the "modern" St. Nicholas was born.

he slumbered for 100 years until Irving awakened him.)

The second creator of the Victorian Santa was the prosperous gentleman farmer and poet Clement C. Moore, who wrote "The Night Before Christmas." Moore lived with his beloved wife, Elizabeth, and their nine children in a big, comfortable Georgian manor house he had inherited on 96 acres in Manhattan, in an area called Chelsea. Early one Christmas Eve, in his carriage en route to Washington Market to purchase a turkey, he began composing a

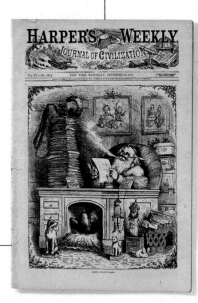

Like the wind he rode upon, Nast's Santa symbolized a powerful and life-giving force in all of us: the joy of giving.

MERRY OLD SANTA CLAUS.

NGRAM SAW DIMJ IN THE ACT OF DESCENDING A CHIMNEY.

HERE HE IS!

A VISIT FROM ST NICHOLAS

ILLUSTRATED BY THOS NAST

McLOUGHLIN BROS NEW YORK

A merry Christmas

A MERRY CHRISTMAS

F.A.O. SCHWARZ

May Kris Krinkle bring the tree
Laden with good gifts for thee.

Christmas poem for his six-year-old daughter, Charity. Back home in his study, he consulted Irving's *History* and finished the poem in three hours. That night, at supper, he read it aloud to his family. "The Night Before Christmas" was an instant hit, first with Charity's Sunday School class, then with the readers of the Troy (New York) *Sentinel*, which published the poem the following Christmas in 1823.

Forty years later, the political cartoonist Thomas Nast immortalized Moore's Santa with his classic drawing of a Santa so "chubby and plump, a right jolly old elf" that "I laughed when I saw him in spite of myself." As cartoonist for the influential illustrated *Harper's Weekly*, for each Christmas issue he drew a Santa, which he claimed was a welcome relief from the relentless pressure of political cartooning. Printed in magazines, on calendars, posters and greeting cards, Nast's Santa has changed

Brilliantly colored chromolithographed "scrap"—holly wreaths, mistletoe, angels and Santas—embellished tree decorations and Christmas cards.

little over the years. Always with a sprig of holly tucked into his furred red cap, a black belt strapped around his four-foot girth, he beams perpetual jolliness to the world—sometimes from a Civil War battlefield, sometimes from a chimney top, or sometimes bending over cherubic children with visions of you-know-what dancing in their heads.

While Santa provided the family tree and the stockings, when it came to gifts he begged assistance and Victorian families leapt to the call. Women's magazines trumpeted the make-it-yourself message across prairie and farmland. In November 1890 one editor, Emma Hopper, reassured readers: "An article that one makes is certainly a more complimentary gift than one bought, for we weave with every stitch sweet wishes for the recipient that untold gold cannot purchase." Her suggestions included a heart-shaped chamois eyeglass cleaner, a photo case made of silk-covered

In medieval Bavaria, St. Nicholas was a messenger who took children's requests to the Christ Child, or Christkindl.

Game of the
VISIT OF SANTA CLAUS

McLoughlin Bros.
New York

COPYRIGHTED 1897

cardboard, a black apron for a lady in mourning—gifts that would be "attractive and dainty and not make inroads on the purse."

America churned out enough pen wipers, calico aprons, knitted mittens, embroidered suspenders and bed slippers, stenciled lampshades, cigar and comb cases, hand-painted collar and button boxes and shoeshine kits to fill a train of boxcars. But no homemade gift could upstage the magic of an imported pink-cheeked bisque doll brought from Paris, or wind-up soldiers from Switzerland that marched and tatted drums, or a miniature steam train from England, fired with naphtha (a mix of gasoline and benzene, and highly inflammable) that spun around a track eight times a minute, tooting the same mournful wail as a real locomotive. The rage in 1890 was a Polyoptican, a sort of VCR in its day, calculated to enchant friends for an evening of parlor entertainment. The Poly-

By the 1870s, St. Nick had become a shameless huckster, beaming generosity from trade cards, lapel buttons, catalogs, calendars, box lids and posters.

GIFTS FOR THE CHRIST CHILD

The first Christmas gift-givers were shepherds, dressed in animal skins, who visited the Christ Child the night of his birth, bringing a cruse of oil, a piece of cheese, and fleece for a blanket. Twelve nights later, having read a special message in the bright star of Bethlehem, three Persian priest-kings came by camel to honor the Child King with gifts of gold, frankincense and myrrh, once used in perfumes and to embalm the dead.

optican magnified images on a wall 400 times. Two hundred titles were available, including "Around the World in 80 Sights," "Portraits of Prominent Persons" and "Illustrations of a Temperance Lesson."

By the 1880s, Santa, now a thoroughly secularized folk hero, was ever ready at the merchant's elbow, prompting Victorians to share their prosperity to the fullest. He appeared on trading cards and calendars, in newspaper advertisements and catalogs. He hoho'd customers into the splendid mercantile palaces of R.H. Macy and A.J. Stewart in New York and John Wanamaker's in Philadelphia. Inside the glass and mahogany doors, the mountains of gift choices grew more glittering year by year. For "the woman desirous of having something better than the standard product," Tiffany's advertised a silver-plated bicycle with ivory handlebars and a jeweled lantern.

ELEGANT AND USEFUL HOLIDAY GIFTS.

THE KING OF THEM ALL.

A VICTORIAN CHRISTMAS LIST

Gift ideas from the *Ladies' Home Journal*, Christmas 1903.

- **For the minister:** a new carriage (a cooperative gift); a magazine subscription; a message of goodwill signed by the congregation.
- **For policemen:** pulse warmers, money.
- **For the washerwoman:** a turkey, a new market basket.
- **For the doctor:** a carriage clock, pocket pencil, cash box for the office.
- **For the only girl in the world:** a framed picture of her favorite author; a gold-plated glove buttonhook; an ostrich feather boa, direct from the producer; handkerchiefs of pale pink, blue, lavender, green or yellow chiffon, which, while "pretty to look at, do not fulfill the first duty of a handkerchief, which is to endure soap and water."
- **For the only man in the world:** a canvas auto coat ("the swellest garment ever designed for stylish dressers, extra-size people easily fitted"); sheet music for "T'aint No Disgrace to Run When Yer Skeered" and "The Heart Breaker Rag"; a lot in Tacoma, Washington, something different, not frivolous for $5 down and $5 a month up to $100.
- **For sons:** a savings bank; a Shetland pony; a Stevens rifle, pistol or shotgun ("For the young of the land, Stevens means safety, accuracy . . . and makes MEN out of BOYS").
- **For daughters:** muff, hair ribbons, fox terrier; a Lustra Painting Outfit, adaptable to "numberless decorative purposes . . . without a tedious course of study or much application."

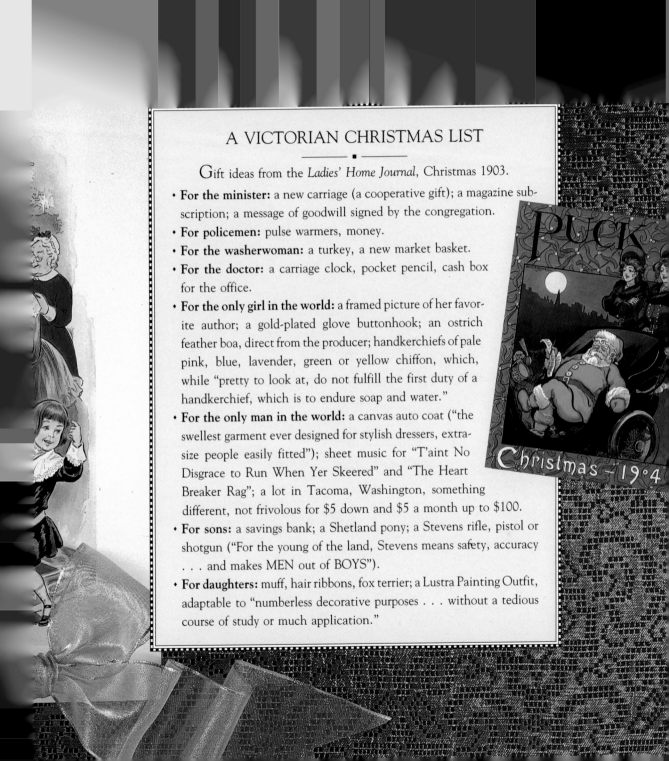

Yes, gift-giving was getting out of hand. Pulpits found themselves in a terrible bind. That it is better to give than receive was clearly an established tenet in the hearts of parishioners, but keeping Christ in Christmas was tricky business. One writer, Helen Prescott Spofford, deplored the state of affairs: "Our Christmas today makes me sometimes fear that the Christmas of our youth is degenerating into a festival of storekeepers. Once there was merrymaking at home, trimming the church with evergreens, the exchanging of gifts whose value was chiefly in their handiwork . . . gradually the increase of wealth has brought about an increase in the cost of gifts, and the storekeepers are quick to set the world aflame every year."

Such was the sentiment in 1890, ruefully echoed a century later.

The final religious barrier to Santa and Christmas fell when Sunday schools enlisted St. Nick as part of their Christmas programs. He rewarded children for Bible memorization, promptness, attendance and deportment.

1905 · Greetings

THEO. GIER CO.

OAKLAND AND SAN FRANCISCO
CAL.

1905	January					1905
Sunday	Monday	Tuesday	Wednesday	Thursday	Friday	Saturday
1	2	3	4	5	6	7
8	9	10	11	12	13	14
15	16	17	18	19	20	21
22	23	24	25	26	27	28
29	30	31				

MERRY
CHRISTMAS
TO ALL

Whether celebrated in the city or country, Christmas festivities in America reflected a rich range of traditions that immigrants brought to their new land from their mother countries.

Beginning with their first settlement in Delaware in 1638, Scandinavians celebrated Christmas with door wreaths and greens, and on December 14 with a candlelight parade honoring St. Lucia, a virgin whose crown of candles symbolized her purity. The French, clustered around New Orleans, dined after midnight Mass at their traditional *reveillon*, a supper crowned with a *bûche de Noël*, a Yule log made of cake and spun-sugar icing dotted with meringue mushrooms.

The Germans, of course, brought their little table Christmas tree, its branches strung with *lebkuchen*

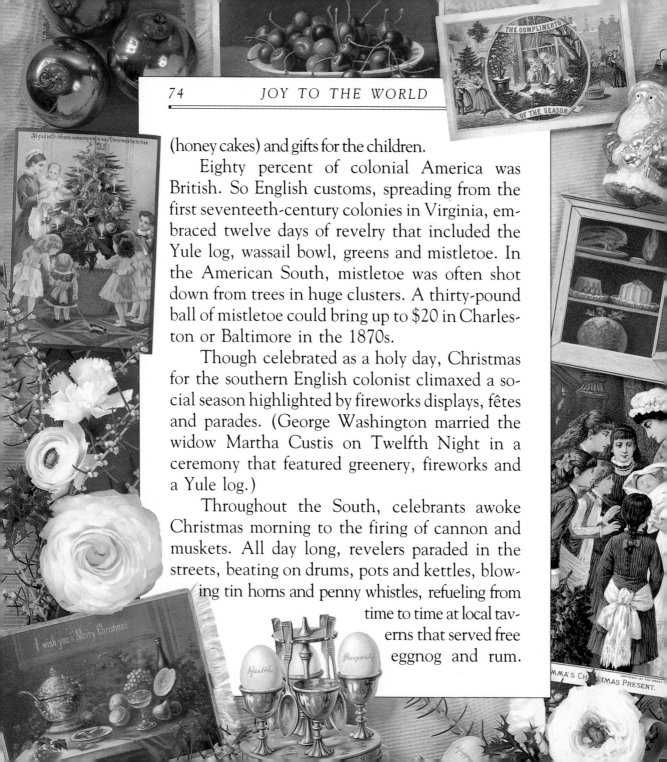

(honey cakes) and gifts for the children.

Eighty percent of colonial America was British. So English customs, spreading from the first seventeeth-century colonies in Virginia, embraced twelve days of revelry that included the Yule log, wassail bowl, greens and mistletoe. In the American South, mistletoe was often shot down from trees in huge clusters. A thirty-pound ball of mistletoe could bring up to $20 in Charleston or Baltimore in the 1870s.

Though celebrated as a holy day, Christmas for the southern English colonist climaxed a social season highlighted by fireworks displays, fêtes and parades. (George Washington married the widow Martha Custis on Twelfth Night in a ceremony that featured greenery, fireworks and a Yule log.)

Throughout the South, celebrants awoke Christmas morning to the firing of cannon and muskets. All day long, revelers paraded in the streets, beating on drums, pots and kettles, blowing tin horns and penny whistles, refueling from time to time at local taverns that served free eggnog and rum.

But it was a young London journalist, Charles Dickens, who established what we now call an old-fashioned, real Victorian Christmas. With his dazzling descriptions of the Christmas feast, the Christmas tree, shops glittering with sweets, the wassail bowl and the glowing warmth of the family circle, Dickens made Christmas irresistible.

A *Christmas Carol*, written in six weeks, completed Dickens' Christmas gift for Victorians. In it, Scrooge, a rich miser, is moved to compassion by human suffering and shares what he has with the modest, hard-working Cratchit family—a sympathetic scenario to a rich Victorian businessman desiring to ease any pangs of conscience wrought by his new wealth.

In 1867 and 1868, when he came to America, Dickens read his works to packed houses. Audiences of 35,000 in New York and Boston cheered him through their tears. A *Christmas Carol* gripped the country like a

fever, and in its way it still does. Year after year the story is read, quoted, and dramatized on stage and television. Is there a grammar school Christmas program that does not end with Tiny Tim sending parents home with his cheery "God bless us, every one!"?

Along with the Cratchit family on that Day of Days, Victorian England dined upon roast goose, a standing rib of beef with Yorkshire pudding, or a boar's head, already dear in 1900 at a cost of $15 to $20 a head. And, of course, plum pudding. So traditionally English is this sloppy "mess of suet, bread crumbs, raisins, liquor and spices" that it has been called the glue of the British Empire. Custom decrees that the pudding must be mixed in late November on the first Advent Sunday, called Stir-Up Sunday, and that each family member have a go at beating the mixture, always stirring clockwise to ensure good luck. After the beating, a ring, a coin, a silver thimble or personal charm are thrown into the thick-

A COLONIAL CHRISTMAS

In the winter of 1609, with only 40 of the original 100 settlers surviving, the English colonists of Virginia feasted at the largesse of Powhatan's sons on "plentie of good oysters, fish, fresh wild foule . . . nor never had better fires in England than in their warm smokie houses."

On Christmas Day, the perfectly round pudding was presented on a silver platter lit with brandy and crested with holly.

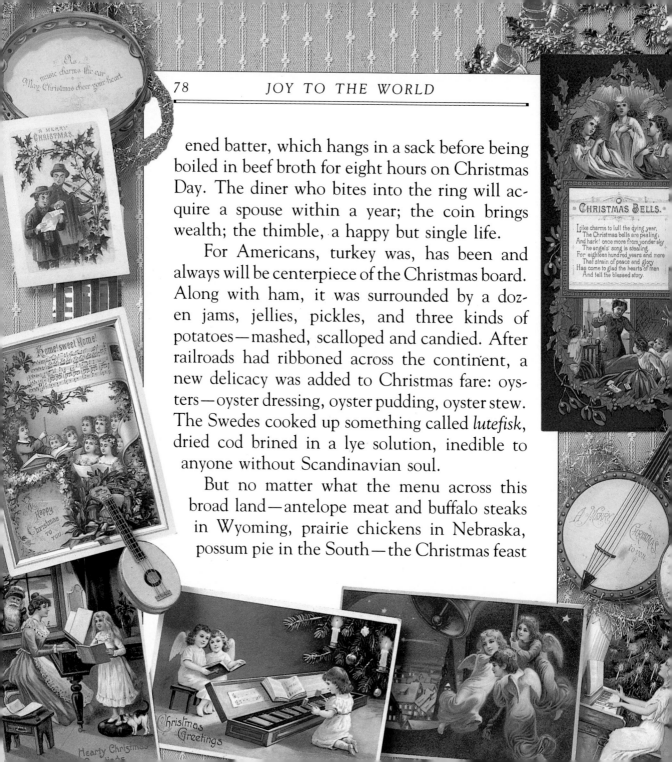

ened batter, which hangs in a sack before being boiled in beef broth for eight hours on Christmas Day. The diner who bites into the ring will acquire a spouse within a year; the coin brings wealth; the thimble, a happy but single life.

For Americans, turkey was, has been and always will be centerpiece of the Christmas board. Along with ham, it was surrounded by a dozen jams, jellies, pickles, and three kinds of potatoes—mashed, scalloped and candied. After railroads had ribboned across the continent, a new delicacy was added to Christmas fare: oysters—oyster dressing, oyster pudding, oyster stew. The Swedes cooked up something called *lutefisk*, dried cod brined in a lye solution, inedible to anyone without Scandinavian soul.

But no matter what the menu across this broad land—antelope meat and buffalo steaks in Wyoming, prairie chickens in Nebraska, possum pie in the South—the Christmas feast was weeks in preparation. Such was the magnitude of holiday gastronomic endeavors that in November 1890 Louise Knapp urged readers in her column, "The Practical Housekeeper," to husband their physical resources. "For hundreds of women, the holiday meals are bugbears," she wrote. "While women should make their tables examples of daintiness and good taste, which applies at no season of the year so forcibly as it does at Christmastide, do not, I pray you, overwork yourself." For Christmas Day she advised serving two meals only, beginning with a "Modest Christmas Breakfast" of "Malaga grapes, Florida oranges, oat flakes and cream; hot rolls, fried oysters, waffles, cream toast, beefsteak, potato chips, big hominy, fried sausage and coffee"—to be followed six hours later by Christmas dinner!

A dinner of eight courses lasting three or four hours was not unusual, even in families of modest circumstances. Only at Christmas were children permitted to eat at their own table, set in the corner of the dining room, and free to frolic in the front parlor between courses—an unheard-of privilege the rest of the year. The

The decision whether or not to hitch up the carriage to the sleigh depended on the depth of the snow, four packed inches being required for a four-person sleigh. Horses were shod with rubbed-cleated horseshoes; children, with clamp-on ice skates. Neither were particularly good insurance against falling on icy roads or snow-drifted ponds.

presentation of the plum pudding was the signal for all children to return to the table. The pudding, ringed in its spectral blue brandy light, illuminated faces rich with anticipation. After a blessing for "all the hands that prepared it," the head of the household sliced the steaming masterpiece with elegant flourishes of an ornate silver knife and serving fork.

After dessert, the children's Christmas crackers—paper favors filled with sweets and trinkets—accompanied glasses of port for the grown-ups. Glasses clinked in re-

CHRISTMAS OLD AND NEW

"Not one of us but can feel the thrill and movement of the time that affects every state of society," wrote Mary Mapes Dodge, editor of *St. Nicholas Magazine*, in 1893. "And yet these are but the tide and waves. Beneath is the infinite ocean of goodness and love. The spirit of Christmas is the same—yesterday, today and forever—and those beautiful old carols are as full of sweetness and cheer now as in olden times."

membrance of absent family members, and in toasts to good fortune for the coming year.

Almost as elaborate as the dinner preparations were the plans for the Christmas program. For weeks, family members consulted and agonized over their contributions. A poem, a song, a recitation? A violin sonata?

All assembled in the front parlor. There was always a lisped rendition from "The Night Before Christmas," recited by the youngest family member, twisting in new velvet breeches. There was the posed tableau of the Nativity, accompanied by the rich, lyrical prose of the Gospel according to St. Luke.

"Christmas won't be Christmas without any presents."
—Louisa May Alcott, Little Women

Christmas
Greetings

A Merry Christmas.

A MERRY
CHRISTMAS

As backdrop for the family Christmas program, a bowl of wassail sizzled on the sideboard. An ancient and beloved English custom, wassail took on certain permutations once it had crossed the Atlantic. Strait-laced New Englanders took the liquor out; free-spirited Virginians put more in. By the end of the century, Prohibitionist Victorians were mulling cider spiced with cloves. But all spluttered with the *de rigueur* roasted apples, quaffed amid rounds of Christmas carols.

By the time children were four feet tall, they knew all verses, sometimes in German and English, to old favorites: *Silent Night/Stille Nacht; O Christmas Tree/O Tannenbaum.* Hardly a Victorian parlor was without its piano or organ—many bought on the installment plan, to be sure, or ordered through a Sears, Roebuck catalog. Piano lessons were an educational staple for a properly bred young lady, and she practiced

Loving Christmas
Wishes.

for her Christmas presentation for weeks.

But the best part of the Christmas program were the parlor games. Handed down for generations was the game of Snap Dragon, a Dickensian favorite, in which players tried to fish as many raisins as possible from a dish ringed with alcohol that had been set aflame. (The winner, with the most raisins, could exact tribute — called a forfeit — from the vanquished.) There was also Blind Man's Buff, and Drop the Handkerchief, Musical Chairs, Puss in Boots, Button Button, Who's Got the Button; charades and the enactment of historical events. Oh, the laughter to see staid Aunt Savana emoting as the dying Cleopatra with an asp at her bosom! Or Grandpa Carlton, rat-a-tat-tatting his imaginary drum as "the shot heard round the world" resounded on the Lexington green.

The cadence of a country Christmas was quite different. In Victorian

Some things never change. Then, as now, children tumbled outdoors with that first glorious snowflake, to build snowmen and snow castles.

A Merry Christmas to you.

“What shall we Buy?”

PAINTING BOOK

Much fun for you

CHRISTMAS BELLS.

B for the Bells
That at Christmas-
time ring.

B

MERRY WINTER TIME

Christmas toys reflect-
ed Victorian goals. For
girls, there were dollhouses
and sewing kits; for boys,
savings banks and model
railroads. For both: building blocks,
Noah's Ark, kittens and puppies.

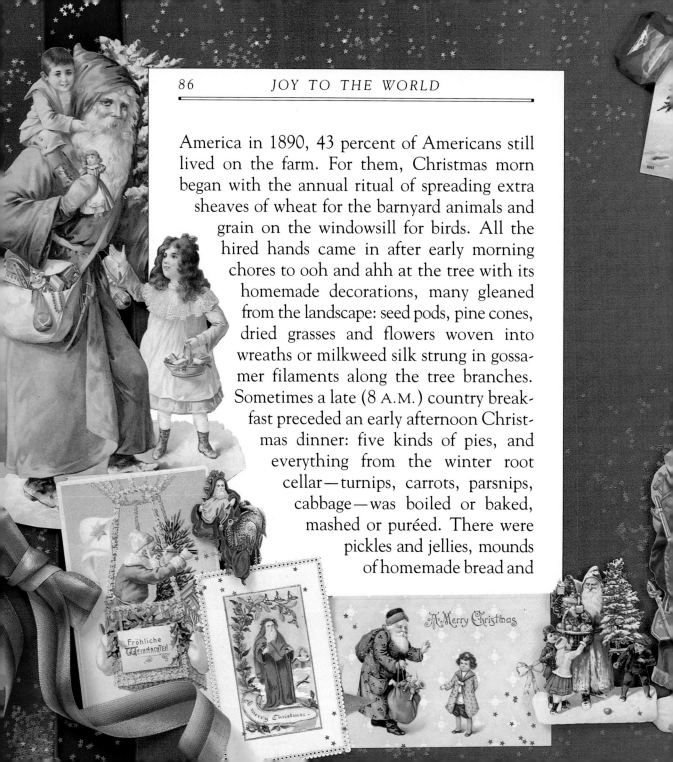

America in 1890, 43 percent of Americans still lived on the farm. For them, Christmas morn began with the annual ritual of spreading extra sheaves of wheat for the barnyard animals and grain on the windowsill for birds. All the hired hands came in after early morning chores to ooh and ahh at the tree with its homemade decorations, many gleaned from the landscape: seed pods, pine cones, dried grasses and flowers woven into wreaths or milkweed silk strung in gossamer filaments along the tree branches. Sometimes a late (8 A.M.) country breakfast preceded an early afternoon Christmas dinner: five kinds of pies, and everything from the winter root cellar—turnips, carrots, parsnips, cabbage—was boiled or baked, mashed or puréed. There were pickles and jellies, mounds of homemade bread and

sweet rolls, homemade beer and beet wine. By midafternoon, children were out on the pond, trying their new skates, or skimming down the hill on new sleds until starlight twinkled them back into the warm glow of the household.

A Christmas Day might also include a visit to relatives, the delivery of dinners to the poor, a candlelit church service or reading aloud from the Bible at home. And finally, at the end of a long day, hugs and kisses under the mistletoe, prayers, and a peek out the window to say good-night to the star of Bethlehem.

Unless otherwise noted, all antique paper ephemera items reproduced in this book were originally printed by the nineteenth-century color process of chromolithography. Descriptions read clockwise, beginning at center top of each page.

Endsheets: Wallpaper pattern, border; Art Wall Paper Mills; flexographic process; c1890. Cigar label, stock blank cartouche; gilded, embossed; Schmidt & Co., N.Y.; c1895. **P. 5:** Wallpaper pattern, ceiling; Art Wall Paper Mills; flexographic process; c1890. Ornament, jointed paper doll (actress Della Fox); 13½"h; handmade dress of printed crepe paper, crinkled crepe paper, lace trimming; c1900. Card; die cut, gilded, embossed border; c1880. **P. 6:** Wallpaper pattern, border; Art Wall Paper Mills; flexographic process; c1890. Handmade ornament; applied die-cut scrap, gold embossed edging on cardboard, flocked, hand cut; c1880. Album card; die cut, embossed; signed E.E. Manly; c1890. Postcard; gold-stamped border, red celluloid applied from behind die-cut window, attached brass greeting; European Post Card Co., N.Y.; c1910. Card; silk-fringed, double-sided, embossed, gilded border, applied chromo; c1885. Scrap; die cut, embossed; c1875. Scrap; die cut, embossed; Raphael Tuck, London; c1905. **P. 7:** Ornament; 19½"h; scrap torso and feet, handmade cotton batting robe over cardboard, crepe paper trim, applied Dresden stars; c1900. Scrap; die cut, embossed; c1885. Buttons; glass, faux gemstones, brass; c1880. Pair of dolls, English; porcelain, in Victorian dress; c1988. Card; foil over embossed, die-cut paper lace, applied chromo, gold leaf; c1880. Scrap; die cut, embossed; c1900. Card folder; silver foil-stamped paper lace, applied chromo center; c1875. Miniature New Year's card; red silk fringe, gold edged; c1875. Card; die cut, embossed, gilded, applied scrap, gold stamped; France; inscribed 1879. Christmas cracker, "U-Neak Snapping Mottoes"; contains favor, hat; crepe paper wrapper, applied cloth leaf, Santa strap; S.D.&N., N.Y.; c1915. Scrap; die cut, embossed; c1875. Card; die cut, embossed, gilded, applied scrap; c1866. Scrap; die cut; c1915. Postcard; embossed, silvered; Germany; c1910. Christmas cracker, "U-Neak Snapping Mottoes"; contains favor, hat; crepe paper wrapper, applied cloth leaf, Santa strap; S.D.&N., N.Y.; c1915. **P. 8:** Doll; bisque; c1900. Foldout card; two levels, seven stages, die cut, embossed, gold-stamped border, assembled scrap figures, chromo die-cut panels; inscribed 1879. Game, "Panorama of The Visit of Santa Claus to the Happy Children"; crayon litho, stencil hand-coloring; metal crank turns continuous roll of pictures between wooden cylinders; box lid: label applied to black embossed paper over cardboard; Milton Bradley, Springfield, Mass.; c1873. Buttons, "Gay Nineties"; brass, faux gemstones; c1890. Play poster; 15½"h × 10¼"w; Milton Bradley; Samuel Bowles, Printers, Springfield, Mass.; c1873. Heart pin; enamel, brass; c1900. Pen; gold agate; c1860. Card case; enamel, hand painting; c1850. Paper doll folder, Santa cover; die cut, easel back; contains little girl paper doll, 5 costumes, toys, hats; S&C; c1910. Wreath pin; glass, brass; c1920. Floral pin; garnet, brass; c1900. **P. 9:** Card; die cut, double-sided image, front shown; England; c1895. **P. 10:**

Booklet, *King Winter*; 20 pp.; Gustav W. Seitz, Hamburg; c1880. **P. 11:** Scrap; die cut, embossed; c1890.

DAY OF DAYS

P. 12: Card; embossed; c1885. Trade card, fancy goods store; Stern Brothers, N.Y.; c1885. Scrap medallions; die cut, embossed; c1880. Card; embossed; c1885. Friendship card; die cut, embossed, applied scrap, ribbon pull tab activates scene of family at table; c1880. Scrap medallion; die cut, embossed; c1880. Card; die cut, embossed; c1885. Card; die cut, embossed border; Marcus Ward, London; c1875. Scrap medallion; die cut, embossed; c1880. Card/candy container; die cut; Raphael Tuck, London; c1895. Trade card, fancy goods store; Stern Brothers, N.Y.; c1885. Ornament; thin-walled, mold-blown glass, silver, applied scrap; c1890. Card; gilded; c1880. **P. 13:** New Year's card; die-cut edge, embossed, gilded; cover with applied scrap pulls open to reveal die cut of children leaning on wall in front of landscape background; c1880. Card; die-cut embossed edge, applied scrap; Goodall, London; inscribed 1873. Card/candy container; die cut; Raphael Tuck, London; inscribed 1894. Postcard; embossed; Paul Finkenrath, Berlin; pmk. 1907. New Year's card/candy container; die cut; Raphael Tuck, London; inscribed 1894. Mechanical card; die cut, embossed edge, gold stamped, applied chromo; shutters open to reveal girl in window; pull tab changes scene, reveals greeting; wheel at bottom changes times of day; c1880. Ornaments; thin-walled, mold-blown glass, hand-colored; c1915. Three-panel foldout card; applied scrap, gold embossed oval, printed silk center applied behind die-cut opening, Dresden star, silk tassel; c1880. Ornament; blown glass beads, wire, silver foil center, applied die-cut scrap; c1910. Card; gilded, silvered border; c1885.

A BRIGHT AND HAPPY CHRISTMAS

P. 14: Carriage trims; red glass prisms, metallic lace with embroidery; c1890. Silver spoon; c1910. Miniature silver tray; c1930. Jubilee souvenir, "The Royal Circle at Windsor (Four Generations)"; mounted on heavy cardboard, gilded edges, easel back with key to figures; boxed (not shown); Raphael Tuck, London; c1885. Paper packages, "Stollwerck's Princess Chocolate"; Stollwerck Bros., Cologne, N.Y.; c1880. Ring; emeralds, diamonds, gold; c1890. Cornucopia ornament; embossed, gilded, applied chromo; c1880. Brooch; moonstone, brassplate; c1910; courtesy Walter's Union Square Shoppes, N.Y.C. Novelty doll; china with walnut body; shell lifts to reveal china baby doll in bassinet; silk and velvet trimming; Germany; c1870. Scrap; die cut, embossed; c1885. Candle holder; tin, wire, clay counterweight ball, gilded, hand-made; c1870. Cotillion badge; foil over embossed, die-cut paper, netting, red gelatin film; c1875. Mechanical New Year's card; pull tab opens doors to reveal waiter with tray; die cut, embossed, gilded; c1880. Bracelet; brass, faux topaz; c1900. Compact; brass, faux gemstones; c1920. Necklace, Hungarian; seed pearls, quartz, brass; c1900.

P. 15: Carriage trims; red glass prisms, metallic lace with embroidery; c1890. Cotillion badge; foil over embossed, die-cut paper, netting, red gelatin film; c1875. Dresden ornament; foil over paper, hand-colored, scrap figures; Germany; c1880. Card; die cut, embossed, gilded border, applied chromo; England; c1875. Scrap; die cut, embossed; c1885. Box; brass, faux gemstones; c1910. Necklace, Hungarian; paste, gilt; c1920. Buttons, "Gay Nineties"; brass, faux amethyst, brass, cut steel; c1890. Scrap; die cut, embossed; c1880. Brass buckle; c1900. Scrap; 13"h; die cut, embossed; c1890. **P. 16:** Advertising novelty (candelabra); one of 3-piece set; cardboard, die cut, embossed, gilded; c1895. Candy container Santa; 14½"h; torso lifts to reveal container; hand-painted face, rabbit fur beard, felt robe, cord sash, woven basket, mica, goosefeather tree, papier mâché, cardboard container, wood base; Germany; c1890. Miniature stuffed bear; c1890. Miniature doll; bisque, cotton crochet; c1900. Candy container Santa; 8½"h; torso lifts to reveal container; hand-painted face, rabbit fur beard, felt robe, gold glitter, mica, goosefeather tree, papier mâché, cardboard container, wood base; Germany; c1910. Advertising novelty (mantel clock); imprinted "Compliments of Hermann Wark, Watchmaker, Engraver and Jeweler"; 15½"h; one of 3-piece set; die cut, embossed, gilded; Germany; c1890. **P. 17:** Advertising novelty (candelabra), one of 3-piece set; cardboard, die cut, embossed, gilded; c1895. **P. 18:** Early cards: Die cut, embossed, applied greeting; c1875. Scrap applied to printed background; c1865. Three-panel foldout; silvered paper lace, die cut, embossed, applied scrap; c1880. Silvered paper lace envelope; die cut, embossed; opens to reveal Father Christmas; Joseph Mansell, London; c1870. Silver pen rest; c1900. Silver pens; c1880. Silver stamp case; c1880. Silver charm; c1900. Early cards: Paper lace, applied scrap, silk ribbon bow, handwritten inscription; England; c1870. Die cut, embossed border, applied scrap; 1863. Die cut, embossed, applied scrap; c1860. Miniature silver candlestick; c1920. Early cards: Embossed paper lace, greeting, scrap, applied to scalloped card; c1870. Die cut, embossed, gilded border, applied scrap; Goodall, London; c1870. Multicolored wood engraving; c1875. New Year's card; embossed lace border, applied chromo; inscribed 1873. **P. 19:** "The First Christmas Card"; J.C. Horsley, 1843; reproduction by De La Rue, London; c1880. Early cards: Die cut, embossed, applied scrap border, mica, cotton batting, dried moss, greeting; c1875. Die cut, embossed, silver stamped, applied chromo; c1875. Embossed, die-cut border, applied paper lace oval, greeting, dried seaweed, mica, scrap, watercolor sky; c1875. Embossed border, applied chromo; c1875. New Year's card; die cut, embossed border; c1870. Chromo of children on sled; c1875. Card; Metamorphic; landscape becomes Father Christmas' face; c1875. Silver card holder; c1890. Early cards: Embossed, gilded border (trimmed); c1870. Embossed paper lace, applied holly and mistletoe scrap; c1875. Three-panel foldout; paper lace, embossed, silvered, imprinted silk center, applied from behind die-cut window; c1880. Card; die cut, embossed, gilded border; silk ribbon pulls down flowers, reveals greetings; c1880.

P. 20: Scrap; die cut, embossed; c1900. Window card, Marcus Ward, London; 9¾"h, 25"w; c1885. Cards; c1885. Robin eating berries; c1880. Silk-fringed, hanging cord and tassels; L. Prang, Boston; c1895. Embossed, applied scrap; Goodall, London; c1860. Embossed; Prussia; c1895. Prize design; Raphael Tuck; c1885. **P. 21:** Card; Goodall, London; c1880. New Year's sachet card; embossed, gilded paper lace, chromo applied from behind die-cut opening; c1875. Scrap; c1875. Card; c1875. Card, "The Kindly Robin"; Castell Brothers, printed in Bavaria; c1895. New Year's card; applied scrap; c1870. Card; silk-fringed; H. Giacomelli, artist; L. Prang, Boston; 1883. **P. 22:** Balloon ornament; glass; c1890. Scrap; 7¼"h × 7¼"w; die cut, embossed; c1890. **P. 23:** Postcard; gelatin surface; Germany; pmk. 1921. Handbag; squash seeds, cut steel beads, silk; c1880. Buttons; glass, brass; c1890. Frankincense. **P. 24:** Scrap; die cut, embossed; c1890. Dresden ornament; embossed gold foil, tinsel; Germany; c1900. Postcard; embossed, gilded; Germany; pmk. 1909. Postcards; Germany; c1910. **P. 25:** Foldout Nativity; 11"h × 9½"w; 5 stages; foil over paperboard, die cut, embossed, scrap, printed tissue behind windows; string unfolds honeycomb canopy when bottom panel is pulled down; c1910. Scrap; 7"h; die cut, embossed; c1890. **Pp. 26–27:** Buttons; blown glass faux pearls; c1890. Scraps; 10"h; die cut, embossed; c1890. Buttons; blown-glass faux pearls, c1890. **P. 28:** Scrap; 7"h × 11"w; die cut, embossed; c1890. Cards; Raphael Tuck, London; c1890. Album card; c1890. **P. 29:** Scrap; 7"h × 11"w; die cut, embossed; c1890.

DECK THE HALLS

P. 30: Mechanical postcard; die cut, embossed; robin folds out, feet turn, cartwheel turns; EAS, Germany; c1910. Scrap; die cut, embossed; c1885. Postcard; embossed; John Winsch; 1910. Scrap; die cut, embossed; c1885. Postcard; embossed; John Winsch; 1910. Boxes; holly paper over cardboard; c1910. Gift tag; embossed, gilded; c1910. Scrap; die cut, embossed, c1885. Advertising calendar (girl sledding); imprinted merchant's name; calendar pad missing; 14½"h × 10¼"w; die cut, embossed; c1910. Scrap; die cut, embossed; c1885. Postcard; embossed; John Winsch; 1910. Scrap; die cut, embossed; c1890. Scrap; die cut, embossed; c1885. Postcard; embossed; c1910. Postcard; gelatin finish, gold stamped; Germany; pmk. 1912. Scrap; die cut, embossed; c1885. **P. 31:** Card; greeting trimmed off; c1885. Scrap; die cut, embossed, c1885. Scrap; die cut, embossed; c1890. Cornucopia; holly paper, applied scrap, tinsel rope; c1900. Dresden ornament; embossed, foil over cardboard, red celluloid center; Germany; c1900. Scrap; die cut, embossed; c1875. Scrap; die cut, embossed; c1875. Scrap; die cut, embossed; 1885. Scrap; die cut, embossed; c1900. Scrap; die cut, embossed, applied silk; c1885. Box; poinsettia/holly paper over cardboard; c1910. Card, "King of the Holly"; De La Rue; c1890. Mechanical card; string causes coins and currency to appear; England; c1890. Scrap; die cut; c1870. Box; holly paper over cardboard; c1910. Scrap; die cut, embossed; c1900. Scrap; die cut, embossed; c1890. **P. 32:** Glass ball ornaments: *Kugels*; embossed brass caps, brass rings; 2" to 6"; Germany; c1870–1900. Scrap; 13"h × 8½"w; die cut, embossed; c1890. Ornaments: Blown glass indent beads, wire, tinsel rope; c1900. Lantern; c1920. Plum; c1920. Double-headed bulldog; c1910. Pendant; wire wrapped; c1920. Beaded; Czechoslovakia; c1920. **P. 33:** Glass ball ornaments: *Kugels*; embossed brass caps, brass rings; 2" to 6"; Germany; c1870–1900. Ornaments: Daisy; c1920. Santa; blown glass beads, wire, applied scrap face; c1890. Cherub; hand painted; c1910. Glass bead star; Czechoslovakia; c1920. Ball pendant; gold ribbon, tinsel, applied scrap Santa. **P. 34:** Ornament; cotton batting, mica frosting, scrap face, Dresden gold-foil wings, buttons; c1910. Scrap; die cut, embossed, c1885. Ornament; cotton batting, mica frosting, scrap face, Dresden foil wings, buttons; c1910. **P. 35:** Ornaments: Boy holding ship, girl holding dog; 17¼"h; scrap torso, feet, cotton batting, crepe paper trim, Dresden foil stars; c1900. Girl jumping rope; scrap face, cotton batting, crepe paper, Dresden foil stars, wire; c1910. Cornucopia; applied scrap Santa face, Dresden foil trim, glazed paper over cardboard, silk ribbon hanger; c1900. Santa; scrap face, hair beard, cotton batting, twig, clove buttons; c1900; courtesy Starr Ockenga. Angel; flat Dresden foil over cardboard, applied scrap face; Germany; c1890. Cornucopia; pattern embossed paper over cardboard, Dresden foil trim, applied scrap of child's face and flower (obscured), silk ribbon hanger; c1900. Santa; scrap face, crepe paper hat, Dresden gold stars, cotton batting, mica frosting, gold cord sash; c1910. Heart; foil over cardboard; Germany; c1900. **P. 36:** Advertising novelty; die cut; Kinney Bros. cigarettes; c1890. Album card; c1890. Advertising novelties; die cut; Kinney Bros. cigarettes; c1890. Ornament; *Kugel*; heavy glass, embossed brass cap; Germany; c1880. Card; mica frosting, c1890. **P. 37:** Advertising novelties; die cut; Kinney Bros. cigarettes; c1870. Magazine illus., "Under the Christmas Tree"; *Die Gartenfaube;* von R. Beyschlag, artist; Max Seeger Lithographer, Stuttgart; 1892. Flat Dresden ornament; foil over embossed cardboard, hand-painted, applied scrap, tinsel; Germany; c1880. Advertising novelties; die cut; Kinney Bros. cigarettes; c1890. New Year's card; L. Prang, Boston; inscribed 1879. Advertising novelties; die cut; Kinney Bros. cigarettes; c1890. Card; c1870. Advertising novelties; die cut; Kinney Bros. cigarettes; c1890. Trade card; Woolson Spice Co.; J.M. Bufford's Sons Lithographers; c1890. **P. 38:** Dresden ornaments; Germany; c1880–1910: Baby in hammock; embossed foil over cardboard, applied scrap, tinsel. Man in moon, trolley (candy container, top lifts off), horse, automobile: foil over embossed cardboard. Elf riding reindeer; foil over embossed cardboard, cotton beard, glitter, goosefeather tree, cloth bag, string, hand-painted. Whale, swordfish, fish (hand-painted), foil over embossed cardboard. Boat; foil over embossed cardboard, cotton smoke. Sailboat; foil over embossed cardboard, cloth, ribbon, string. Small boot (candy container); gilded, embossed, cloth bag with drawstring. Boot (candy container); foil over embossed cardboard, gold flashing, remnant of silk lining. Slipper (candy container); velvet, glazed paper over cardboard, silk lining, silk bag with drawstring, die-cut embossed trim. Chest (candy container, lid lifts); glazed paper over cardboard, gold-foil embossed edging. Basket (candy container); cloth-covered cardboard, gold-foil embossed, silk ribbon, paper lace trim inside. Elf; foil over embossed cardboard, felt carrot with feather stem. Harp; foil over embossed cardboard, silver cord. Basket (candy container); foil over embossed paper, silk-lined. Baby carriage; foil over paperboard, embossed, applied scrap, flashed. Clock; foil over embossed paperboard; flashed; applied printed face. Clown; papier-mâché, hand-painted, wool hair, silk ribbon, foil over embossed paperboard medallion. Banjo (candy container, top lifts off); embossed foil over cardboard, painted cardboard, brass keys, string, ribbon hanger. Chest with handle (candy container, lid lifts); foil over embossed cardboard. **P. 39:** Dresden ornaments; Germany; c1880–1910: Butterfly; foil over embossed cardboard, glitter. Lion; embossed cardboard, glass eyes, ivory teeth. Ram; foil over embossed cardboard. Star; crepe paper, foil on embossed paper, tinsel, gelatin film. Squirrel, fox; foil over embossed cardboard. Elephant; foil over embossed cardboard, silk ribbon. Condor; foil over embossed cardboard, flashed. Rooster; foil over embossed cardboard. Peacock; foil over embossed cardboard, flashed. Swan; foil over embossed cardboard. Swan pulling shell, shell, frog, alligator, turtle; foil over embossed cardboard, flashed. Fish; foil over embossed cardboard. Two fish; foil over embossed cardboard, flashed. Three horses pulling sleigh; foil over embossed cardboard, string reins. Stag; embossed cardboard, hand-painted, glass eye. Moose, buffalo, camel; embossed cardboard, hand-painted. Beetle; foil over embossed cardboard, hand-painted. **P. 40:** Postcard; embossed, gilded; c1910. Postcard; hold-to-light; D.R.G. Germany; pmk. 1908. Beaded mistletoe; c1890. Gift tag; die cut, embossed; c1910. Postcard; hold-to-light; D.R.G. Germany; pmk. 1908. **P. 41:** Calendar fan; die cut, embossed paperboard, gilded, cord with tassels; 1911. Postcard; embossed, gilded; John Winsch; 1910. Scrap; die cut, embossed; c1900. Gift tag; die cut, embossed; c1910. Cornucopia candy container; printed paperboard; cloth ribbon; c1915. **Pp. 42–43:** Fan calendar; die cut, embossed, gilded, ribbon, cord with tassel; inscribed 1899. **P. 44:** Stockings: 24"h, lithographed on glazed cloth; c1910. 28"h, lithographed on cloth; c1895. **P. 45:** Postcards: Embossed, gilded; c1910. Embossed, gilded; pmk. 1910. Illus. from children's book; c1910. Scrap; die cut; c1910. Card; Walter Crane, artist; c1895. Trade card; Woolson Spice Co.; Cosack, Buffalo, N.Y.; c1890. Scrap; die cut; c1910. Stock illus.; imprinted "J.B. Barnaby & Co."; multicolored wood-engraving; Jno. A. Haddock; c1879. Postcard; embossed, gilded, silvered; John Winsch; 1912. **P. 46:** Card; S. Hildesheimer; 1883. Advertising giveaway print, "A Christmas Dream"; Union Pacific Tea Co.; ad copy on back; 1887. **P. 47:** Pyramid Picture Blocks; chromolithographed paper over wood; c1910. Postcard; embossed, gilded, c1910. Trade card; imprinted "The Trojan Santa Claus, Wm. H. Frear, Troy Bazaar"; Wells, Sackett & Rankin, lithographers, N.Y.; c1890. Stock card; imprinted "A Happy Christmas"; J. H. Bufford's Sons Lithographers,

Boston; c1885. Postcard; embossed; Raphael Tuck, London; inscribed 1910.

SANTA AND THE SPIRIT OF GIVING

P. 48: Advertising foldout calendar; Theo. Gier Co.; 7¾"h × 14½"w; die cut, embossed, gilded; mica frosting, calendar pad; 1903. **P. 49:** Postcards: embossed, gilded; pmk. 1907; gilded; Germany; c1910; gilded; Germany; c1910; embossed, gilded; International Art Publishing Co., N.Y.; pmk. 1906; Germany; c1910. Buttons; brass, paste; c1890. **P. 50:** Scrap; 10"h × 6¾"w; c1890. Album card; die cut, embossed; c1895. Scrap; die cut, embossed; c1895. Scraps; die cut, embossed; c1885. Card; double-sided, silk-fringed; Annie Simpson, artist; c1895. Card; embossed, gilded; c1885. Scraps; die cut, embossed; c1885. Card; L.B. Comins, artist; L. Prang, Boston; 1888. Scrap; die cut, embossed; c1895. Hidden-message card; die cut, embossed, gilded border; scrap composition lifts to reveal greeting; c1880. Album card; c1890. Card; die cut, embossed, gilded, silvered, applied chromo; c1870. Card; die cut, embossed, gilded, envelope flap lifts to reveal greeting; c1875. Scraps; die cut, embossed; c1885. Scrap; die cut, embossed, gilded, silvered; c1880. Card; die-cut embossed border, applied chromo, greeting; c1875. Scrap; die cut, embossed; c1895. **P. 51:** Album card; c1895. Scrap; die cut, embossed; c1885. Scrap; die cut, embossed; c1875. **P. 52:** Sachet; embossed, silvered, printed silk center applied behind die-cut opening, applied embossed gold ornament; c1875. Folder pages, cover; "Christmas and His Little Friends"; gilded; Marcus Ward, England; c1885. Shaped card; engraved, hand-colored; Robinson Engraving, Boston; 1882. Scrap; die cut, embossed; c1875. Greeting card; c1875. **P. 53:** Hidden-message card; gilded, applied chromo lifts to reveal greeting; B. Sulman, London; c1870. Cards: gilded; J. Mansell, London; c1875. Scrap; die cut, embossed; c1875. Folder pages; gilded; Marcus Ward, England; c1885. Scrap; die cut, embossed; c1875. Hidden-message card; die cut, embossed, gilded, applied scrap lifts to reveal greeting; inscribed 1875. Card; gilded; England; c1875. **P. 54:** Scrap; die cut, embossed; c1920. Postcard; Rafael Neuber, Vienna; c1899. Scrap; die cut, embossed; c1875. Postcard; embossed; M. Ettlinger, London; pmk. 1905. Postcard; Rafael Neuber, Vienna; c1899. Scrap; die cut, embossed; c1875. Postcard; Germany; pmk. 1899. Postcard; Rafael Neuber, Vienna; c1899. Postcard; embossed, gold stamped; EAS, Germany; c1910. Scrap; die cut, embossed; c1900. **P. 55:** Children's book illus., Thomas Nast, artist; McLoughlin Bros., N.Y.; c1895. Scrap; die cut, embossed; c1875. Postcard; embossed; Paul Finkenrath, Berlin; pmk. 1910. Postcard; embossed; Germany; pmk. 1912. Scrap; die cut, embossed; c1920. Postcard; embossed, gilded; Paul Fink enrath, Berlin; pmk. 1908. Postcard; embossed, gold-stamped; EAS, Germany; pmk. 1908. Chromo; trimmed; c1875. Postcard; gold stamped; S.B., Germany; c1910. Postcard; embossed; Paul Finkenrath, Berlin; c1910. Scrap; die cut, embossed; c1915. Scrap; die cut, embossed; c1905. **P. 56:** Cover illus., *Harper's Weekly*; wood engraving; Alfred Fredericks, artist; Harper and Brothers, N.Y., Dec. 31, 1870. Cover illustration, "Santa Claus's Mail", *Harper's Weekly*; wood engraving, Thomas Nast, artist, Harper and Brothers, N.Y., Dec. 30, 1871. Cover illus.; *Illustrated London News*, Christmas Number, two-tone wood engraving, signed "A.H."; London; 1876. **P. 57:** Illus., "Merry Old Santa Claus"; *Harper's Weekly*; wood engraving, Thomas Nast, artist; Harper and Brothers, N.Y., Jan. 1, 1881. Magazine illus., "Santa Claus"; *New Mirror*; steel engraving; Sherman & Smith; 1844. Magazine illus., "St. Nicholas, on his New Year's Eve Excursion"; wood engraving, R. Roberts, engraver; N.Y.; Jan. 2, 1841. Children's book, *Visit from St. Nicholas*, 24 pp., 6 illus., Thomas Nast, artist; McLoughlin Bros., N.Y.; c1868. Magazine ad; Ives, Balkeslee & Co.; Santa wood engraving; 1883. Children's book illus., *London Toy Warehouse* (trimmed), wood engravings, hand-colored; England; c1840. Shaped transformation; trade card; cover lifts to reveal Santa; imprinted "D. McCarthy & Co.'s Dry Goods and Fancy Goods"; T. Newcomb, lithographer, N.Y.; 1882. Small woodcut; trimmed; 1880. **P. 58:** Scrap; 11¼"h × 8½"w; die cut, embossed; c1890. Postcard; gold stamped; Germany; pmk. 1909. Postcard; embossed, gold stamped, pmk. 1907. Scrap; die cut, embossed; c1890. Stock trade card; imprinted on back, "S.B. Thing & Co., Shoe Store"; c1895. Scrap; die cut, embossed; c1885. Trade card; F.A.O. Schwarz; Meyer, Merkel & Ottmann Lithographers, N.Y.; c1880. Scrap; die cut, embossed; c1885. Hidden-message card; gilded; applied Santa scrap lifts to reveal greeting; Marcus Ward, London; c1880. Carriage trims, tassels and fringe; metallic threads, glass beads; c1890. Scrap; die cut, embossed; c1890. Postcard; embossed; pmk. 1906. Scrap; die cut, embossed, mica chips, easel back; c1900. Scrap; die cut, embossed; c1910. **P. 59:** Chromo; 12"h × 7"w, die cut, embossed; c1890. Scrap; die cut, embossed; c1885. Postcard; embossed, gold-stamped; c1909. Scrap; die cut, embossed; c1900. Scrap; die cut, embossed; c1900. Postcard; embossed, gold-stamped; Germany; c1910. Scrap; die cut, embossed; c1900. Die cut; embossed; c1895. Scrap; die cut, embossed; c1885. Card; c1890. Scrap; die cut, embossed; c1900. Postcard; deckle edge; pmk. 1923. Scrap; die cut, embossed; c1910. Die cut; embossed; c1885. Carriage trims, tassels and fringe; metallic threads, glass beads; c1890. **P. 60:** Postcard; applied real hair beard, mica chips, Dresden stars; J.W.B. Germany; c1905. Scraps; die cut, embossed; c1895. Scrap; 11¾"h; die cut, embossed; c1890. **P. 61:** Scrap; 10"h, die cut, embossed, mica chips; c1890. Postcard; gelatin finish, gold stamped; Saxony; pmk. 1910. Scrap; 10"h, die cut, embossed; c1890. **P. 62:** Board, spinner, hand-painted lead playing piece; playing piece; "The Game of Kriss Kringle's Visits"; 1898. Board, playing pieces, "Game of the Visit of Santa Claus"; hand-painted lead, turned wood; 1897. Box lid, "Game of the Visit of Santa Claus"; 19¾"h × 10½"w; paper label, paper-wrapped cardboard; McLoughlin Bros., N.Y.; 1897. **P. 63:** Box lid, "The Game of Kriss Kringle's Visits"; 15"h × 22⅛"w; paper-wrapped cardboard, applied label; McLoughlin Bros., N.Y.; 1898. Box lid, "Santa Claus Game"; 15"h × 9"w; paper-wrapped cardboard, applied label; Parker Brothers, Salem, Mass.; c1910. Spinner, board, playing pieces, "Santa Claus Game"; c1910. Candy container; Santa head top lifts off; papier mâché, hand-painted face, cotton beard, felt hood, chenille trim, cardboard base; c1910. Ball container; paper-wrapped cardboard; wood-grained paper lining; c1880. Board, spinner, "Game of the Visit of Santa Claus"; 1897. **P. 64:** Trade card; Wm. H. Frear's Troy Cash Bazaar; c1885. Transformation trade card; sleeping child folds down to reveal Santa holding toys; Ehrichs' Holiday Goods; crayon litho; Burrow-Giles Lithographers, N.Y.; 1882. Advertising buttons; celluloid, pin backs: Bon Marché, Farmers Trust Co.'s Xmas Club, Quackenbush's, Marshall Field's, McCurdy's, Jordan Marsh Co.; c1900–10. Trade card; 13½"h × 7¼"w; crayon litho, embossed; Geo. Heather Fancy Goods, N.Y.; c1890. Card; c1885. **P. 65:** Trade card; Holmes & Co., Famous English Biscuits; crayon litho, trimmed; Donaldson Brothers Lithographers, Five Points, N.Y.; 1879. Toy catalog, price list; Milton Bradley, Springfield, Mass.; 28 pp.; letterpress, wood engravings; 1873–74. Card; c1885. Trade card folder; Max Stadler & Co., Clothing; 3-color litho; Mayer, Merkel & Ottmann Lithographers, N.Y.; 1885. Advertisement; Elgin watches; clipping, *The Aldine*, N.Y.; wood engraving; 1872. Trade card folder; G.A. Schwarz's Toy Bazaar, Philadelphia; 1880. Advertising button; Bon Marché, Seattle; celluloid, pin back; c1910. Back cover of preceding trade card folder. **Pp. 66–67:** Double spread magazine illus., "The King of Them All"; *Puck*, Ehrhart, artist; c1900. **P. 68:** Scrap; 10½" × h 11½-w; die cut, embossed, mica chips; L.D. & Co.; c1890. **P. 69:** Advertising foldout calendar; 11¼"h × 12½"w; Theo. Gier Co., Oakland, San Francisco, Cal.; 3 stages, die cut, embossed, mica chips, calendar pad; 1905.

MERRY CHRISTMAS TO ALL

P. 70: Advertising display piece, "Drink High Spy"; 17½"h × 15"w; die cut, embossed; 1895. New Year's postcard; embossed, gold stamped; Germany; c1910. Card; gilded; c1885. Postcard; embossed; Germany; pmk. 1915. Foldout novelty advertising card, "Punch and Judy Show"; Sprague Warner, packaged foods and coffees, Chicago; 3 stages, die cut, embossed; Raphael Tuck, London; c1895. New Year's postcard; embossed; Paul Finkenrath, Berlin; pmk. 1904. Advertising novelty; Kinney Bros. cigarettes; c1895. New Year's postcard; embossed, gold stamped; Germany; c1910. Advertising novelty; Kinney Bros. cigarettes; c1895. Card; gilded; c1885. **P. 71:** Advertising novelty; Kinney Bros. cigarettes; c1895. New Year's card; gilded; c1885. Dresden ornament candy container; top lifts off, paper over cardboard, painted cardboard, gold-embossed trim, string, ribbon hanger; Germany, c1900. Card; die cut, embossed, gilded, applied chromolithograph; c1875. Mechanical foldout; 7 stages, die cut, embossed border, scraps, applied chromolithographed background; pull tab activates mechanism; c1880. Scrap; die cut, embossed; c1875. Advertising novelty; Kinney Bros. cigarettes;

c1895. Greeting card; die cut, embossed gilded border; c1865. New Year's postcard; embossed, gilded; S.L., Germany; inscribed 1908. Dresden ornament; silver foil over cardboard, embossed gold-foil leaves, paper label; Germany; c1895. New Year's card; embossed border; inscribed 1874. Card; Goodall, London; c1875. Card; die cut, embossed border; Goodall, London; inscribed 1875. Advertising novelty, "Fun and Frolic"; imprinted "C.D. Kenny Co. Teas"; 4 panels, die cut, embossed; Raphael Tuck, London; c1910. Christmas card; c1870. Dresden ornament; foil over embossed cardboard, gilded, flashed; Germany; c1890. Card; gilded; c1875. Santas; chenille on wire; c1910. Dresden ornament candy container; top lifts off, satin over cardboard, gold trim, painted cardboard, string; Germany; c1910. Dresden ornament; foil, paint over cardboard, paper label, silk ribbon bow; Germany; c1900. Demitasse cups; ornate silver; c1880. New Year's postcard, "Ladies Calling Day"; embossed, gilded; Germany; pmk. 1910. Card; embossed border, gilded; c1875. Card; die cut, embossed, gilded border, applied background, scrap figure, greeting; c1875. Card; gold background; H. Rothe, London; inscribed 1882. Dresden ornament candy container; end pulls out; embossed card board, applied embossed foil leaves and spigot, stick legs, gold cord; Germany; c1900. **P. 72:** Stock advertising calendar; 17″h × 10¼″w; blank, die cut, embossed, gilded, glitter; Germany; c1905. **P. 73:** Scrap; die cut, embossed; c1885. Card; die cut, embossed border; inscribed 1877. Scrap; die cut, embossed; c1890. Scrap; die cut, embossed; c1885. Ornament; scrap head and shoulders, lace bonnet, silk thread bow, linen christening dress and bow, lace trim, homemade; c1900. **P. 74:** Card; silk-fringed, double-sided; Raphael Tuck, London; c1880. Card; Baxter process; c1870. Figurative glass ornament; thin-walled, mold-blown, hand-painted; c1920. Card; door opens to reveal food; Birn Brothers, London; printed in Germany; c1890. Trade card, "Mamma's Christmas Present"; Great Atlantic & Pacific Tea Company, Teas and Coffees, N.Y.; c1895. Card; die cut, center egg removable; Raphael Tuck, London; c1895. Card; silk-fringed, double-sided, gilded; c1875. Card; England; c1875. *Kugels*; embossed brass caps, brass rings; Germany; c1880. **P. 75:** Postcard; embossed; Germany; c1910. Thin-walled, mold-blown glass ornaments: Boat; Santa scrap, wire wrapped; c1910. Bell; c1920. Figural Santa; hand-painted, mica chips; c1920. *Kugel*; embossed brass cap, brass ring; c1880. Postcard; embossed; c1910. Postcard; embossed, gilded; Germany; pmk. 1908. Mechanical postcard; opening cover activates foldout scene of family around tree; 3 stages, die cut, embossed; c1908. Card; die cut, embossed border; Goodall, London; c1875. Ornaments: *Kugel*; embossed brass cap, brass ring; Germany; c1880. Lantern; thin-walled, mold-blown glass, hand-painted, c1920. Real photo postcard; c1910. *Kugel*; embossed brass cap, brass ring; Germany; c1880. **P. 76:** Card; gold background; Walter Crane, artist; England; c1890. Scrap; die cut, embossed; c1885. Small plate; porcelain; c1900. Decorative miniature tree; 5½″h; goose feathers, tinsel, gelatin film, scrap, blown-glass beads, dried berries, painted wood base; c1885. Card; c1875. Card; embossed border; c1870. Miniature tray; ornate silver; c1880. **P. 77:** Scrap; 11⅜″h; die cut, embossed; c1900. Postcard; embossed, gilded, applied silk; Germany; c1910. Card; gold border; c1890. Miniature candelabra; c1900. Card; c1885. Card; embossed, gilded; Germany; pmk. 1910. **P. 78:** Card; L. Prang, Boston; 1878. Ornament; die cut, tinsel rope; c1890. Dresden ornament candy container; top lifts off; paper over cardboard, printed scene, painted cardboard, string; Germany; c1900. Postcards: Embossed, gilded; pmk. 1914. Embossed; c1910. Hold-to-light; c1905. Germany; 1910. Embossed; Germany; c1910. Dresden ornament, candy container; top lifts off; silk over cardboard, painted cardboard, gold trim, string; Germany; c1910. Card; c1885. Card: c1870. Ornament; die cut, tinsel rope; c1890. **P. 79:** Dresden ornaments; Germany; 1880–1910: Flat wreath; foil over embossed paperboard, flashed. Lyre; foil over embossed cardboard, gold cord. Harp; gold foil over embossed cardboard, silver foil strings. Mandolin candy container; top lifts off; paper over cardboard, gold-embossed trim, painted cardboard, string, ribbon hanger. Postcard; embossed, gilded; S. Langsdorf, Germany; c1910. Postcard; embossed; Germany; c1910. Scrap; c1875. Flat Dresden ornament; embossed, foil over paperboard; Germany; c1890. Dresden ornament candy container; top lifts off; silk over cardboard, gold trim, painted cardboard, string; Germany; c1910. Christmas ornament; die cut, tinsel rope; c1890. Card; Hildesheimer & Faulkner, England; printed in Germany; 1890. Angel with bell; celluloid, brass; c1920. Scrap; uncut sheet, foil over embossed paperboard, flashed; c1920. **P. 80:** Scrap; embossed, die cut; c1890. Scrap; die cut, embossed; c1890. **P. 81:** Trade card; imprinted on reverse "Hodgson & Smith, Ranges and Stoves. Stafford Springs, Ct."; c1895. Dresden ornament; foil over embossed cardboard, ribbon; Germany; c1890. Card; c1880. New Year's card; embossed border, c1870. Lapel pin, ice skate; brass; c1900; courtesy Walter's Union Square Shoppes, N.Y.C. Scrap; die cut, embossed; c1890. Scrap; die cut, embossed; c1890. Scrap; c1900. **P. 82:** Postcards: Embossed; Paul Finkenrath, Germany; c1908. Embossed; Paul Finkenrath, Germany; pmk. 1908. Mechanical, pull tab activates revolving celluloid disk with snow; embossed; Germany; c1910. Embossed; Paul Finkenrath, Germany; c1908. Embossed; Germany; c1910. Embossed; Paul Finkenrath, Germany; 1910. **P. 83:** Scrap; embossed, die cut, mica chips; c1890. Card; De La Rue, London; c1880. Postcard; embossed; Paul Finkenrath, Berlin; c1910. Scrap; 11¼″h × 10″w; die cut, embossed; c1890. **P. 84:** Card; illus. seen through die-cut window; die cut; embossed cover lifts down to reveal greeting; c1895. Children's book, *Christmas Bells*; 16 pp., chromolithographed paper laminated to cardboard, cord bound; De Wolfe Fiske, Boston; c1895. Paperboard toys, "Animals and Their Riders"; from set of 10 jointed, stand-up animals with 10 interchangeable riders; die cut, embossed; Raphael Tuck, London; c1910. Children's book, *Merry Winter Time*; 12 pp., die-cut cover; Faudel Phillips & Sons (with Raphael Tuck trademark), London; c1900. Scrap; die cut, embossed; c1890. Trade card; Richard Schwarz Toy Emporium, Boston; Mayer, Merkel & Ottman Lithographers, N.Y.; c1890. Half-penny doll; c1890. Children's book, *What Shall We Buy?*, Father Tuck's "Little Artists" series; 20 pp., color illustrations of objects with corresponding line drawings for coloring, perforated for removal; Raphael Tuck, London; c1900. Paperboard toy; from a series of Noah's Ark animals; die cut, embossed, joined together by paper springs; Raphael Tuck, London; c1900. **P. 85:** Stock card; imprinted on back "Hyde Park Clothing Co."; die cut, embossed; c1895. Box lid, "Kriss Kringle Picture Cubes"; patterned paper wrapped over cardboard, paper label; McLoughlin Bros., N.Y.; 1896. Half-penny doll; c1890. Children's book, *Around the World with Santa Claus*; 16 pp.; R. André, artist; McLoughlin Bros., N.Y.; 1881. Scrap; die cut, embossed; c1890. Children's book, *Santa Claus Toy Shop*; 12 pp., printed on linen, McLoughlin Bros., N.Y.; c1915. Scrap; die cut, embossed; c1890. Paperboard toys; from series of Noah's Ark animals; die cut, embossed, joined together by paper springs; Raphael Tuck, London; c1900. Paperboard toy, "Animals and Their Riders"; from set of 10 jointed, stand-up animals with 10 interchangeable riders; die cut, embossed; Raphael Tuck, London; c1910. Picture blocks, "Kriss Kringle Picture Cubes"; 6 different illus.; paper applied over heavy cardboard; McLoughlin Bros., N.Y.; 1896. Scrap; die cut, embossed; c1910. **P. 86:** Scrap; die cut, embossed; c1890. Postcard; embossed; L.&B., Germany; c1910. Card; die cut, embossed border, red and purple silk figure, paper face and hands, figure applied to rice paper panel, the whole hand-painted and applied to card, gilt trim; N. Genoux, Paris; c1880. Scrap; die cut, embossed; c1875. Postcard; die cut, embossed; Germany; c1910. Scrap; 10¾″h × 6″w; die cut, embossed, paperboard; c1905. **P. 87:** Scrap; 9½″h × 6¼″w; die cut, embossed; c1910. Postcard; Germany; pmk. 1911. Buttons; brass, gilt metal, faux amethyst, paste, cut steel; c1880. Postcards: Hold-to-light; D.R.G.M., Germany; pmk. 1909. Embossed; inscribed 1912. A.&M.B., Germany; pmk. 1910. Embossed, gilded background; G.G.R., Germany; c1910. Embossed, gilded; Germany; pmk. 1914. Buttons; brass, gilt metal, faux amethyst, paste, cut-steel; c1880. Trade card; Woolston Spice Co., Ohio; c1895. Scrap; die cut, embossed; c1910. Scrap; die cut, embossed; c1895. Postcards: Gelatin finish; A.A., Germany; pmk. 1913. Imprinted on back with postcard dealer's offer; Harrisburg Post Card Factory, Harrisburg, Pa.; embossed; S.O., Germany; c1910. Embossed, gilded; Germany; pmk. 1910. **P. 88:** Necklace; faux pearls, gilt metal, paste; c1930. New Year's cards; 1885. Button; mother-of-pearl, brass; c1880. New Year's card; die cut, embossed border; c1875. Button; enamel, brass; c1880. Cotillion badge; foil over embossed die-cut paper, silk ribbon, netting, applied gold stars; c1875. Scrap; die cut; c1875. New Year's cards: "A Happy Round of Months"; prize design; silk-fringed, double-sided (Christmas subject on reverse); signed EAL; S. Hildesheimer; c1885. Die cut, embossed, gilded border, applied scrap; c1895. Button; glass, brass; c1880. New Year's card; die cut, embossed, gilded border, applied chromo; c1875. Cotillion badge; foil over embossed, die-cut paper, silk ribbon, netting, applied gold stars; c1875.